Church Leadership Series

Persuasion

How to Help People Decide for Jesus

Mark Finley

Nampa, Idaho | Oshawa, Ontario, Canada
www.pacificpress.com

Cover designed by Gerald Lee Monks
Cover photo from SermonView.com

Copyright © 2016 Pacific Press® Publishing Association

Published by Pacific Press® Publishing Association
Printed in the United States of America
All rights reserved

The author assumes full responsibility for the accuracy of all facts and quotations as cited in this book.

Scripture quotations taken from the Amplified® Bible, Copyright © 1954, 1958, 1962, 1964, 1965, 1987 by The Lockman Foundation. Used by permission.

Scriptures quoted from RSV are from the Revised Standard Version of the Bible, copyright © 1946, 1952, 1971 by the Division of Christian Education of the National Council of the Churches of Christ in the U.S.A. Used by permission.

Additional copies of this book can be obtained by calling toll-free 1-800-765-6955 or by visiting http://www.adventistbookcenter.com.

ISBN 978-0-8163-6176-2

May 2016

Contents

	Introduction	4
1	The Technique: ABCs of Decision	7
2	The Agent: Power of the Word	12
3	The Psychology: How the Mind Works	17
4	The Benefits: Fanning the Flame of Desire	25
5	The Motivation: Negative and Positive Motivators	32
6	The Impact: Importance of Influence	37
7	The Attraction: Jesus—the Significant Other	42
8	The Process: The Clear and Set Principle	47
9	The Understanding: Perceptual Patterns	53
10	The Indispensable: Visitation Strategies	57
11	The Appeals: Increasing Results	69
12	The Intercession: Prayer Dynamics	79
13	The Hurdles: Overcoming Bad Habits	85
	Conclusion	91
	Bibliography	94

Introduction

Veteran evangelist, J. L. Shuler, used to tell the story of how Henry Ford repaired the car of King Francis Joseph II of Austria, while vacationing in England. While meandering through the English countryside, Henry saw a Ford broken down beside the road. The passengers stood helplessly around. Henry stopped and asked if he could be of help. "Why, yes," said a distinguished-looking man Henry recognized as Francis Joseph. The King did not recognize Henry. But Henry Ford opened the hood of the car he had built and knew so well.

"Crank it," Henry told one of the King's attendants. After listening to the rough-running engine for a few moments, Henry tapped it with a hammer. To the king's amazement, the engine began to run as if it had just come from the factory. "How much do I owe you?" he asked with delight.

Ford responded, "One hundred silver shillings, please."

"One hundred silver shillings?" Francis Joseph repeated unbelievingly. "For two minutes' work?"

"No," replied Ford. "Two silver shillings for two minutes' work, but ninety-eight silver shillings for knowing where to hit!"

Knowing where to hit, knowing where and how to call for decisions for Christ, Shuler emphasized, is the key to successful soul winning. This book is about the science of decision. Too often pastors, Bible instructors, lay people, and even evangelists seek decisions without understanding the basic principles that motivate decision. The soul winner must know the human mind—how people think, why they act, and the skills necessary to know where to hit.

I have read books on decision that seem manipulative. This is not such a book. Page after page it emphasizes cooperation with Jesus Christ through the Holy Spirit. He wants to lead His creation to decision. We can hinder Him or we can help him.

It is not sufficient to proclaim the message, or even to convince people that the doctrines are true. The whole purpose of the message we preach is to lead men and women to obey Christ. Our commission from the Lord is not merely to warn men, but to make disciples of all men, to make Christians. That should be our sole objective. We're not merely to convert; not merely to give the message that Christ is coming, but to make people prepared for the Lord. . . . It is at this point (leading to decision) that many a ministry otherwise strong is lamentably weak. More public efforts fail on this point than on all others combined.
—J. L. Shuler
Public Evangelism, p. 180.

The following pages are dedicated not to failure, but to success. Knowing where to hit is the key.

Continuing Education Credit

To qualify for one unit of Continuing Education credit, complete all assignments outlined at the end of each chapter. To apply for CE credit complete the CEU Registration Request on page 95.

1

The Technique:
The ABCs of Decision

When Jesus called us to follow Him in His work for humanity, He promised to teach us how to work with Him "Follow me, and I will make you fishers of men" (Matt. 4:19). Fishers of fish and fishers of men are not born; they are made. And the making begins with observing the Master at work.

In His ministry for souls, what Jesus *was* counted as much as what He *said*. Decisions were made, not only because of the facts He presented, but because of the man He was. Jesus won hearts through relationships as well as through truth. He identified with people. Persuasion involves both *logos* (knowledge) and *ethos* (confidence).

A person's feelings may be positive or negative. Negative feelings can lead to a negative decision. Thus, not only message and messenger but method is critical in getting a positive decision. *How* we speak truth affects results; so does *when* we speak truth. A Messianic passage brings the above elements together:

> *The Lord God hath given me the tongue of the learned, that I should know how* **[method]** *to speak a word* **[what is said]** *in season* **[when it should be said]** *to him that is weary: he wakeneth morning by morning, he wakeneth mine ear to hear as the learned. The Lord God hath opened mine ear, and I was not rebellious, neither turned away back* **[the kind of person Jesus was]**.   —Isaiah 50:4, 5

Each morning, in answer to His Son's prayer, the Father revealed the "necessary wisdom" to secure positive decisions. The Father will also teach us what to say, how to say it, and when to say it. Some of us have not learned.

"I'm so excited with the truth," a convert told me. "I've shared your tape on the mark of the beast with my Catholic relatives."

The wrong message. The wrong time. The wrong way. And certainly a setback in relationships.

Speak "the truth in love," advised Paul (Eph. 4:15). That's

God's way to present beautiful truth through loving people. Decisions are rooted in interpersonal relationships. The more confidence one has in the messenger, the deeper the relationship established, the more likely there will be a positive decision.

Let's follow Jesus and observe Him using the *ABCs of decision*.

A—Acceptance. Jesus accepted men and women where they were. He ministered to them in the condition in which He found them. He did not work for change before establishing a relationship of confidence. He meets a woman of Samaria at a well. He establishes confidence by asking a favor when His countrymen would not even speak to a Samaritan. At the Pool of Bethesda Jesus meets a physical need before seeking a decision. With Nicodemus He consents to a private night meeting to preserve the privacy of the seeking Pharisee.

There are two ingredients in acceptance: agreement and approval.

1. *Agreement.* In seeking decisions, first find areas of agreement. A small agreement will open the way to larger agreements. To seek a decision by saying, "I disagree with you" fractures a relationship before it has had time to "set"; and broken relationships lead to negative decisions. A wise lady put it well:

Agree with the people on every point where you can consistently do so. Let them see that you love their souls, and want to be in harmony with them so far as possible. If the love of Christ is revealed in all your efforts, you will be able to sow the seed of truth in some hearts; God will water the seed sown, and the truth will spring up and bear fruit to His glory. —E. G. White, *Evangelism*, p. 141

For example, an individual says, "I am looking forward to the rapture when earth's problems will be solved, and we will be caught up to meet Jesus." Your response might be "I too look forward to Jesus' return and the final end of sin. It's exciting to sense we are living at the end time." Although you may not agree with your friend on the manner of Christ's return, you surely do agree with him on the fact of Christ's return. Certainly there will be time to share straight forward Bible truth after a trusting relationship has been established.

2. *Approval.* When onlookers condemned Mary for "wasting" expensive ointment on His feet, Jesus praised her for her kindness. He told her her act would be remembered through the centuries as a symbol of loving kindness. Jesus complimented the centurion by declaring, "I have not found so great faith, no, not in Israel" (Matt. 8:10). "O woman, great is thy faith," He said

admiringly to the Canaanite woman (Matt. 15:28). Repeatedly Jesus demonstrated acceptance by agreeing (when He could), by approving, by complimenting, and by appreciating.

Jesus even found ways to express approval of those who had reservations about Him. Speaking of a scribe who had been questioning Jesus, Mark 12:34 states, "When Jesus saw that he answered discreetly, he said unto him, 'Thou art not far from the kingdom of God.'" Jesus looked for a good point. He demonstrated approval. Don't be repelled by negative attitudes or actions on the part of others. They should not have to approve of you before you can approve of them. Do not appear shocked. Demonstrate genuine acceptance. Attempt to agree with them on every point possible. Look for something that you can express appreciation for, and then through little confidences and compliments, attempt to build a bond of unity. Remember, *you manifest acceptance by agreement and approval.*

To demonstrate acceptance of others, get them talking about themselves, their home, the town they live in, their work, family, or business, ideas, accomplishments, background, hobbies, or sports. Be genuinely open to learning from them and they will become open to learning from you. Your accomplishments should always be secondary and subordinate. The wise man put it this way: "Let another man praise thee, and not thine own mouth; a stranger, and not thine own lips" (Proverbs 27:2).

Be a good listener. Pierre Salinger, biographer of John Kennedy, described the interviews Kennedy had when he was President of the United States. He stated that Kennedy had the capacity to sit behind his desk and give you his full, undivided attention for the fifteen to thirty minutes that you were in his presence. Salinger says that Kennedy asked deeply penetrating questions about the topic, as if he completely identified with your needs and had nothing else to do but ask you about your point of interest. No wonder John F. Kennedy was loved by so many people!

Jesus accepted men and women where they were and began to build bonds of friendship that later would be bridges over which the truth could march into their minds.

B—Belief. This is the second key principle of our ABCs. Nobody is won by a person they do not like. Nobody likes a person they feel does not accept them. You must believe that individuals sincerely desire truth and want to follow Jesus, that they are winnable to Christ and His cause, that they are honest and desire to make the right decision. If you believe that men and women are hardhearted, unresponsive, and unreachable, your own attitude will be reflected in the decisions they make.

Andrews University conducted a study of more than 8,300 Seventh-day Adventists in North American, including 320 different churches. Those churches and individuals who believed men and women were winnable were growing the fastest. The survey stated:

> *Some have called it the self-fulfilling prophecy syndrome, but simply put, there is a strong correlation between a pastor's belief that his church can grow and the degree to which it does grow. Those pastors, and we might add as well, church members, who rated their church's growth potential highest were experiencing rapid growth in membership.*
> —"Major Church Growth Study Completed,"
> *Institute of Church Growth Newsletter* February, 1981

Jesus also illustrates this belief principle. He saw people not only as they were, but as they could become. When He looked at the woman at the well. He saw, not an outcast coming from the lower level of society, but a woman who had been hurt and bruised, and He reached out in love. Jesus saw Peter, not as a rough and outspoken fisherman, but as a mighty preacher. He saw Joseph of Arimathea, not as a sophisticated, wealthy businessman, but as a master who loved his servant. He saw Nicodemus, not as a leader of the opposition filled with religious bigotry, but as one who desperately needed to have a new heart. Jesus saw the best in people. He believed in them, and He confidently expected them to make a decision to follow Him.

Here is a Bible trivia question for you. Who was the first missionary Jesus ever sent out? Peter. . . John. . . The 12 apostles. . . The Seventy. . . No! Guess again! The first missionary Jesus ever sent out was a mad man turned messenger—a lunatic turned disciple. Jesus saw in a wild, long haired, raving, screaming demoniac enormous potential for the Kingdom of God. Converted, he became a powerful witness. In fact, he did a work even the disciples were unable to do. What a God! What a Saviour! He constantly transforms the most unlikely prospects, sending them out to touch others with his healing love.

C—Confidence. In leading men and women to decisions for the Master it is imperative that we act confidently, as if it were impossible for us to fail or be disappointed. Expect the person to make the decision. People often act the way we expect them to act. Have you ever noticed that when you smile at people they nearly always smiles back? Friendliness begets friendliness, trust begets trust, and confidence begets confidence. Christ believed in people and anticipated a positive response. He brought out the best in them. Thus they rose to His expectations.

The book of Acts records the greatest church-growth explosion in history. Acts 2 says 3,000 were baptized on the Day of Pentecost. Acts 4 indicates that the church swelled to 5,000 shortly thereafter. If you add women and children, that would mean at least 7,000 to 10,000 believers. Moving through the book we read, "The church throughout all Judea and Galilee and Samaria . . . was multiplied" (Acts 9:31, RSV). Again, "You see, brothers, how many *thousands* there are among the Jews of those who have believed" (Acts 21:20, RSV, emphasis supplied). The Greek word is "myriads," and it means tens of thousands. Astounding growth! Why?

Here's one of their secrets: "Be it known therefore unto you, that the salvation of God is sent unto the Gentiles, and that *they will hear it*. . . . Preaching the kingdom of God, and teaching those things which concern the Lord Jesus Christ, *with all confidence*, no man forbidding him" (Acts 28:28, 31). Like Jesus, the early church taught with confidence—confidence in the Holy Spirit that wherever He sent them He would be present to impress hearts; confidence in people, that they would hear and make right decisions.

Putting it all together, to be a successful soul winner: *accept* men and women as they are by being agreeable and expressing approval; *believe* that they are sincere and genuine; *confidently* expect them to make right decisions. Put these ABCs of decision into practice and watch God work through you.

Continuing Education Assignment

1. Jesus won people through what He was as well as what He taught. Which characteristics of your personality, working in conjunction with the Holy Spirit, have you found most helpful in persuading people to decide for Christ?

2. Which characteristics attitudes have been preventing people from deciding for Christ?

3. Decisions are rooted in interpersonal relationships. People are not won to Christ by a person they do not like. Review one of your recent soul winning contacts and list what you did or could have done to establish a warm personal relationship.

2

The Agent:
Power of the Word

George Whitfield once spent a delightful evening in the home of an affluent couple. Retiring to this room, he was deeply perplexed because they had not yet accepted Christ. Kneeling amidst the lavish surroundings of his room, he asked God to help him know how to reach this wealthy couple.

Next morning, Whitfield noted the lady's diamond had been left on the nightstand beside his bed. Picking it up he scratched on the windowpane, "One thing thou lackest." Without saying a word to her about what he had done, he thanked her for her hospitality and departed.

As she entered his room to tidy up, the sun shone through the window and illuminated those four words. She knew that they were words from the Bible, yet did not know where they were found or their meaning. She was angry at first. Calling her husband she said, "Whitfield has written on our window 'One thing thou lackest.' What do we lack? We don't lack anything. If we did we would buy it. What does he mean?"

Together that night the couple pored over the Scriptures, and after considerable time found the four words in the story of Christ and the rich young ruler. Pondering that story, they understood the meaning of the words and, indeed, found that although they had everything, they had missed the One who *is* everything. Together that night they knelt on their beautiful, plush carpet beside their expensive furniture and dedicated all their possessions, but most of all, their hearts, to Jesus Christ. Four words of Scripture, impressed on Whitfield's mind by the Holy Spirit, changed their lives.

The Bible is God's dynamic agency for soul winning. No man or woman can be effective as a soul winner unless they know how to use the right text at the right time to generate decisions. Paul says, God's Word "is . . . powerful, and sharper than any two-edged sword, piercing even to the dividing asunder of soul and spirit" (Heb. 4:12).

At Creation, the audible Word of God carried with it such power that it generated matter. "By the word of the Lord were the heavens made; and all the host of them by the breath of his mouth (Ps. 33:6). Ellen White declares:

> *The creative energy that called the worlds into existence is the Word of God. The Word imparts power; it begets life. Every command is a promise; accepted by the will, received into the soul, it brings with it the life of the Infinite One. It transforms the nature and recreates the soul in the image of God* —Education, p. 126

The life-giving promises and principles of the Word of God carry with them the power to do that which they declare. Since God's Word is living, it not only presents the way to live, but it carries with it the power to accomplish right living. Ellen White asserts this principle:

> *So with all the promises of God's Word. In them He is speaking to us individually, speaking as directly as if we could listen to His voice. It is in these promises that Christ communicates to us His grace and power. They are leaves from that tree which is "for the healing of the nations." Rev. 22:2. Received, assimilated, they are to be the strength of the character, the inspiration and sustenance of the life. Nothing else can have such healing power. Nothing besides can impart the courage and faith which give vital energy to the whole being.*
> —The Ministry of Healing, p. 122

No book carries as much power as the Word of God for enabling men and women to make decisions; no method is as powerful as taking the texts of the Bible and applying them in real-life situations. In talking to a person about making a decision, one might say, "In my opinion," or "I think," or "My church teaches." But these expressions carry little weight. However, when you and I can open our Bibles and read a text that tells people what God says, that shares with them the will of Christ for their lives, we have enlisted powerful agencies for change.

A former Seventh-day Adventist attended a series of meetings I held some years back. As we visited in her home one evening, I talked to her about returning to the family of God. Her eyes glistened as she replied, "I'd like to, but I can't. I smoke."

I called her by name and asked, "Do you believe that Jesus wants you to have victory over this habit?"

"Oh, yes, I do. But I can't. I'm just too weak."

I said, "May I read you a Bible text?" And I opened my Bible to 1 John 5:14, "This is the confidence that we have in him, that, if we ask any thing according to his will, he heareth us."

"Now, Mary, do you have confidence that you can quit smoking?"

"No."

"Good. Because the Bible says, 'This is the confidence we have in Him.' So where is the confidence?"

"In Him."

Then I read the text once more adding, "If we ask anything according to His will, except to give up smoking, he heareth us." Turning to Mary I asked, "Should I write that in your Bible? Can I have your Bible to write it there?"

She said, "No, it doesn't say that. It says that if we ask *anything* according to His will, he heareth us."

"Is it according to God's will for you to quit smoking?"

"Yes, it is."

"Then, can you ask Christ in confidence for the power He has promised?"

"Oh, yes, I believe I can."

"Now one more question. When will you receive this power to give up smoking? Will it be in a week, a month, three months? When will you receive that power?" Opening my Bible, I turned to John 1:12 and read, "As many as received him, to them gave he power to become the sons of God."

"To receive Jesus is to receive the power," I continued. "Now, tonight we've seen that you can have confidence in Jesus. We've seen that whatever we ask according to His will, He will give us. And we know it's His will for you to give up smoking. We've seen as well, that as you receive Him, you receive power."

Mary sat quietly, a new light coming into her eyes. "Would you like, tonight, to kneel here and tell Jesus that you have confidence in Him to do for you what you can't do for yourself?" I asked. "Would you like to tell Him that you believe it is His will for you to quit smoking and that you'd like to receive power right now, believing by faith that He is giving it to you? And that in spite of any craving, through the power of Christ you'll have victory, in spite of any drive or desire, because His word says it? By faith would you like to believe what God says?"

And so we knelt, and Mary prayed. That night, over eight years ago, God gave Mary total victory over smoking two to three packs of cigarettes a day. Certainly I suggested some principles, such as deep breathing, walking, and water to aid in breaking the habit. But through claiming the promises in the Word of God she found true deliverance in Christ.

"It is not our arguments which God has promised to bless, but His word" (*The Art of Personal Witnessing*, p. 24). I may have debated with Mary on the necessity of her giving up smoking. I might have argued with her that smoking was wrong. Yet I sensed that she already was filled with guilt regarding her smoking and that her great need was the hopeful promises of God's Word.

As men and women come in contact with the Word of God, they are changed. It is possible to read the Bible with a closed mind and receive little benefit. Nevertheless, when men and women seek to know the truth of God, even if at first they may be quite skeptical, coming in contact with the living Word transforms them.

C. S. Lewis began reading the gospels skeptically, yet became charmed by the Christ that he found there. He revealed his changed attitude in the book, *Surprised by Joy*. In that book C. S. Lewis describes how the living Christ transformed him as he read the Scriptures.

Robert Morrison brought his skeptical attitude to the Bible in an attempt to discredit the resurrection of Christ. But as he compared the historical evidence with the biblical account he wrote that marvelous book, *Who Moved the Stone?*, in which he acclaimed the resurrection as a divine event. Morrison was transformed as he read the biblical record.

More than 100 years ago, William Ramsey, a young English scholar, went to Asia Minor with the express purpose of proving that the history given by Luke in his gospel and in Acts was inaccurate. His professors had confidently said that Luke could not be right. Ramsey began to dig in the ancient ruins of Greece and Asia Minor, testing for ancient terms, boundaries, and other items which would expose Luke if he had invented his history at a later date, as the professors claimed. Ramsey compared his archaeological and historical findings with the New Testament account and became so convinced that New Testament Scripture was accurate to the tiniest detail that he became a Christian and a great New Testament scholar. Brought into contact with the living Word and comparing with an open mind the historical evidence, Ramsey was changed.

The successful soul winner must feed on the promises of God's Word. Fixing those promises and principles in memory will enable the soul winner to have an effective approach in meeting others. Dr. C. L. Goodale summarizes:

No man can have a message big enough for souls in need who had not fed upon the word of God until it appears in every drop of his blood and

in every breath which proclaims the message that God has given him.
—*Motives and Methods of Modern Evangelism,* p. 46

And Ellen White emphasizes:

They, (the ministers) do not become more and more efficient in the work because they do not become more and more intelligent in the Scriptures of truth. —*Review and Herald,* April 8, 1890

No doubt you are reading this book because you want to be a more successful soul winner for Christ. Then you must fill your mind with the precious promises of God's Word. Memorize texts on salvation, the second coming of Jesus, the Sabbath, the state of the dead, the sanctuary, the Spirit of Prophecy, the true church, and the essentials of the Advent faith.

Discover those passages that are particularly designed to help people come to Jesus (Matt. 11:28; John 6:37, 38); that show them the joy of forgiveness (Isa. 1:18; 1 John 1:9); that help them know there is power in Christ to change their hearts (2 Cor. 5:17; Heb. 10:8-10); that tell them Jesus has power that enables them to cope with temptation and sin (Heb. 7:25; Phil. 4:13), that help them believe Christ will supply all their needs (Phil. 4:17, 18; Matt. 6:26-33).

These passages are like seeds. Planted in the soil of the mind, they sprout and bear fruit to the glory of God. The seed has life-giving, transforming, life-changing power. Plant it in the soil of minds and there will be an abundant harvest of souls through your ministry. The Bible—the authority of its word and the power of its message—brings decisions.

Continuing Education Assignment

1. What relationship does God's spoken Word in creation have to the Bible in leading men and women to decisions for Christ? (See Hebrews 4:12; Psalm 33: 6, 9.)

2. List what you believe to be the ten most helpful decision texts in the Bible, along with a few words summarizing what each teaches or what question it answers. You could use the ten in this chapter, but might prefer others. Remember, these are *decision texts* not doctrinal texts.

3
The Psychology:
How the Mind Works

A mother took her children to the ice cream store, and the ice cream man asked, "Chocolate or vanilla?"

"Why don't you have more flavors?" the mother replied. "I get so tired of these two."

"Lady," the ice cream man sighed, "If you knew how much time it takes them to make up their minds between chocolate and vanilla you'd never add another flavor."

Some decisions in life are relatively unimportant, like a decision between chocolate and vanilla ice cream. Yet, the power of choice is a God-given faculty. It is absolutely essential that soul winners understand the place of the will in decision-making. The will is the master key of decision.

The ocean liner, Queen Elizabeth, weighs approximately 85,000 tons, yet is guided by a rudder weighing only 65 tons. The rudder, though small compared to the rest of the ship, still controls its direction. The wills of a men and women are the rudders of their lives. It is not the soul winners' prerogative to manipulate the will. It is not their responsibility to force it. Yet they will not succeed in soul winning until they understands how the Holy Spirit relates to it.

> *What you need to understand is the true force of the will. This is the governing power in the nature of man, the power of decision, or of choice. Everything depends on the right action of the will.*
> —*Steps to Christ*, p. 47

> *Through the right exercise of the will, an entire change may be made in the life. By yielding up the will to Christ, we ally ourselves with divine power. We receive strength from above to hold us steadfast. A pure and noble life, a life of victory over appetite and lust, is possible to everyone who will unite his weak, wavering human will to the omnipotent, unwavering will of God.* —*The Ministry of Healing*, p. 176

Every decision that is made, whether it be to buy a vacuum cleaner, or to accept Bible truth and become a Seventh-day Adventist Christian, involves four basic levels.

The first is *information*. This level is where an individual begins to accumulate facts regarding the decision to be made. In deciding to buy a new car, for example, a person shops around, gathering information. The perspective buyer looks at the advantages or disadvantages of purchasing various models, comparing facts on performance, gas mileage, comfort, and affordability. The information level provides opportunity for the gathering of the facts needed to move toward a more intelligent decision. Right decisions won't be made in life unless an individual has right information.

To call for a decision before there is adequate information creates barriers in the human mind, and at that point the will makes a negative rather than positive decision. Therefore, in leading men and women to decisions, it is necessary to ask the following questions: Does the individual have adequate information to make the decision? Is the individual intelligently informed regarding the decision I am asking him/her to make?

There are two significant concepts to observe here if we are going to be effective in helping people decide for Jesus. The first is information overload. Information overload occurs when an individual receives too much information too quickly. If this happens they will not only resist the information but reject the one giving it to them. This is precisely why so many people who attend our evangelistic meetings are thrilled initially when they hear messages on topics like the second coming, salvation, and the origin of evil; but once the testing truths unique to Seventh-day Adventist Christians are presented such as the Sabbath, healthful living, the state of the dead, hell, tithe, and the true church they drop out of the meetings. The problem is information overload. Here are two things you can do to avoid erecting these barriers of resistance:

1. Present testing truths gradually. If possible do not present three or four new truths back to back in the same week.

2. Visit people in their homes immediately after the presentation of testing truths to clear up any major questions. This reduces frustration.

A second major factor in inhibiting decisions is the psychological phenomena of *programmed non-response*. Programmed non-response occurs when the individual hears truth but does not act upon it. A classic example is television. The average 14 year-old boy witnesses 12,000-15,000 brutal murders a year on television. This overdose of violence leads to the repression of the compassionate quality of kindness in helping those who are hurt. The mind and emotions are moved to respond in a positive way, and when an individual does not respond, the ability to do so is lost. To preach for a decision, to inform the intellect and stimulate the emotions but not to appeal for a response hardens a person in their desire not to respond. Here are two ways to avoid programmed non-response.

1. Make regular systematic appeals including hand-raising, kneeling, standing, and altar calls.

2. Use response cards often. The response or decision cards provide an individual the opportunity to respond privately. Once you receive the response card, visit the individual to affirm this positive decision, answer questions, and encourage the person to act immediately.

The second step in the decision-making process is *conviction*. After gathering information, an individual begins to sense what seems to be the right decision in the particular situation—what really ought to be done. In a decision for Christ, an individual's conscience suggests, "This is what I believe God wants me to do. This is what I believe is God's will. If I fail to take the appropriate action I will be outside of God's will."

When a person is under conviction, on the positive side there is the deepening sense of rightness by taking the appropriate action, and on the negative side there is the deepening sense of guilt by not taking that action. On the other hand, decisions usually are not made just because a person is convicted to do something. Some may have a conscience so sensitive that if they are prompted by a sense of rightdoing, and plagued by a sense of wrongdoing, the right decision will be made. Yet, the third level of decision is crucial.

The third level is *desire*. In the desire stage people sort out their own feelings, identify not merely what ought to do, but what they wants to do. "You can lead a horse to water, but you cannot make him drink." But salt can.

Place a block of salt next to the water, let the horse lick the salt, and soon it will become so thirsty it will want to drink. Salt awakens desire.

As soul winners, we are the salt of the earth. It is necessary to present the gospel to men and women in such a way that, not only will they have adequate information and be convicted, but they will want to act on it.

By presenting the benefits of rightdoing, the consequences of wrongdoing, and the influence that the action will have upon others, desire is heightened. Throughout the Bible God, Himself, presents the joy of heaven, the terrors of hell, and His own love as a powerful motive to heighten our desire.

The fourth step, is *action*. When conviction and desire are heightened, an individual acts. Thus the key to the final action is to go beyond information to conviction and desire. J. L. Shuler puts it this way:

> *Decisions stem out of the interplay of knowledge, conviction, and desire in a person's mind. When a person's knowledge, conviction, and desire in reference to a given subject reach a certain intensity, the human mind moves into decision and action in regard to it. Since knowledge, conviction, and desire lead to decision, the sermons, the Bible studies, and the personal talks should be an artful interweaving of the factors of desire and conviction in respect to the given subject. This is needed for bringing about the requisite interplay of knowledge, conviction, and desire for acceptance, decision, and action. As we analyze certain texts we discover that some are especially designed to bring knowledge, others to bring conviction, and still others to bring desire. And often the same text has in it the elements of all three. We need to focus on these texts that will implant conviction and at the same time arouse desire for accepting and following God's great principles as we present them in our Bible studies to the student.*
> —Securing Decision, Part II, p. 1

Implanting conviction

Conviction comes when an individual has adequate information. *But your having given information does not mean your listener has received it.* If the information is clear and free from major obstacles and apparent contradictions, God, through the Holy Spirit, brings about conviction. But information will not lead to conviction unless that information is *clear*. As you move from information to conviction, it is a good rule to preface your first questions with, "Is it clear?"

Giving a Bible study on the second coming of Christ, for example, I desire to plant the conviction that Christ is coming soon. So I might review the study in two or three minutes, saying: "John, *is it clear* to you that when Christ comes He's coming in the clouds of heaven with all the angels so that every eye can see him? Do you believe in your heart that we're living in the last days?" If the response is negative, I must back up and give more information before moving on to conviction. Receiving a positive response, however, I might go on:

"John and Mary, do you hear the voice of Christ calling you to give up anything that would separate you from Him? 1 John 3:2, 3 says, 'Beloved, now are we the sons of God, and it doth not yet appear what we shall be: but we know that, when he shall appear, we shall be like him; for we shall see him as he is. And every man that hath this hope in him purifieth himself, even as he is pure.'

"Do you sense the conviction that God is calling you to totally surrender yourself to Him to prepare for His coming? Would you like to kneel here tonight and make that kind of decision?"

In a study discussing the Bible Sabbath, I might use expressions like this: "Peter, *is it clear* to you that the seventh-day Sabbath is Saturday, the last day of the week, and that God rested on that day? Do you see that God requires us today to keep the Bible Sabbath? Do you sense that the Sabbath is part of God's Ten-Commandment Law?"

After receiving positive responses, I might continue by using Revelation 22:14, "The Bible says, 'Blessed are they that do his commandments, that they may have right to the tree of life, and may enter in through the gates into the city.' Do you hear the voice of God calling you to keep His commandments so that you might enter that city? Do you sense that this is what you ought to do? Would you like to kneel down and pray that God will help you to have the strength to do it?"

Thus conviction has taken place not simply as a person has listened to Bible texts, but as the person has *actively* responded to questions regarding obedience to the Word of God. It is important to emphasize here that the questioning must not be of a threatening nature. The idea is not to intimidate but to discover the person's understanding and views of material presented. Also, emotional questions requiring vague answers, such as, "Isn't the Sabbath truth wonderful?" ought to be avoided. This type of questioning will only result in a defensive response or a passive nod of assent.

Specific questioning allows you to discover the objections in the minds of the people. Since any objection will prove to be an obstacle to conviction, this questioning process is extremely important. Without it, conviction is undefined both in the mind of the person you are working with, and also in your own understanding of his/her views and feelings. So on any topic, we ask a series of questions that may be phrased like this: "Is it clear to you that Jesus is coming soon? Is it clear to you that the Bible

Sabbath is Saturday? Do you believe that your body is the temple of the Holy Ghost? Have you ever understood before our evangelistic presentation that baptism is by immersion?"

Each question is designed to reveal both a personal understanding of, and belief in the topic presented. Seek specific answers that fall into a "yes" or "no" format. Once the student answers these questions positively, read conviction texts that reveal the action God requires and the seriousness of ignoring such directives. Here are a few examples:

Conviction Texts and Appeals
1. *Personal Salvation.* "John, the Bible says, 'All have sinned, and come short of the glory of God' (Rom. 3:23). In Acts 4:12 it says, 'There is none other name under heaven given among men, whereby we must be saved' except Jesus Christ. Do you sense that the only way to be saved is through Christ? Knowing that without Him men and women are eternally lost, would you like to open your heart to receive this Christ tonight?"

2. *Second Coming.* "The Bible teaches that when Jesus returns, you and I will see Him coming. Revelation 1:7 tells us that 'every eye shall see Him.' If you and I are going to greet Him with untroubled minds and joyous hearts, we must do everything now that we know is right. Do you understand that the only way to meet Jesus in peace is to allow Him, through His Holy Spirit, to take out of your life any habit that would separate you from Him? 1 John 3:1-3 points out that those who meet Jesus have had a change in their hearts and lives—they have been born again. Would you like to ask God to take any habit out of your life that would keep you from meeting Him in peace?"

3. *Sabbath.* "As we have studied the Sabbath together have you begun to feel a deepening conviction concerning what God wants you to do? Do you more clearly understand what God expects? Do you see that the Sabbath is part of the Ten Commandment Law? Do you hear God calling you to keep the Sabbath? Do you see that the Sabbath is required for Christians today who love Jesus Christ and that true obedience is a necessity for Christians? The Bible says, in 1 John 2:4, that if we say we follow Christ and are not obedient, we are liars and the truth is not in us. Obedience is the test of the Christian life. Would you like to show your obedience to Christ by keeping His Sabbath?"

4. *Healthful Living.* "The Bible teaches that our bodies are temples of God. But it teaches, as well, that God desires us to keep those bodies pure and holy. 1 Cor. 3:16, 17 says, 'Know ye not that ye are the temple of God, and that the Spirit of God

dwelleth in you? If any man defile the temple of God, him shall God destroy; for the temple of God is holy, which temple ye are.' Do you want to show your love for Christ by keeping your body pure?"

5. *Baptism.* "The Bible says, in John 3:5, 'Except a man be born of water and of the Spirit, he cannot enter into the kingdom of God.' In Mark 16:16, it says, 'He that believeth and is baptized shall be saved.' Would you like to express your belief in Christ by immersion baptism?"

To understand the workings of the human mind, and to cooperate with the Holy Spirit as it works on that mind, is to succeed in getting decisions for Christ. Robert Oliver said,:

He who would influence the judgments of men must first and foremost and finally know the inner recesses of their minds.
—*The Psychology of Persuasive Speech,* p. 6

Ellen White summarizes the entire principle:

In order to lead souls to Jesus there must be . . . a study of the human mind. —*Testimonies for the Church,* vol. 4, p. 67

Every gospel worker needs to understand clearly how the human mind works in making a decision.

You can be an effective soul winner. With your Bible open, supply men and women with clear and accurate information. Assist them by supplying answers to their questions. Read texts which will produce deepening conviction. Do not hesitate to show them what God wants them to do and tell them it is God's will for them to do it. Reveal to them the benefits of right action, the consequences of wrong action, and invite them to make decisions. Blending information, conviction, and desire, prompt them to action.

In our next chapter we'll discuss how to fan the flame of *desire.*

Continuing Education Assignment

1. In giving a series of Bible studies, what percentage of your time do you feel you should spend at each of the four levels of decision? What percentage of your time have you actually spent?

Level	Should Be	Actual
a. Information	_____%	_____%
b. Conviction	_____%	_____%
c. Desire	_____%	_____%
d. Action	_____%	_____%

2. Moving from information to conviction, it is a good rule to preface your first question with what three words?

4

The Benefits:
Fanning the Flame of Desire

Joan had attended the Seventh-day Adventist Church faithfully for two years. She had completed a series of Bible studies, attended a Daniel Seminar, and gone through two full-length Prophecy Lecture Series. But for some reason she had never made a decision to become a Seventh-day Adventist. Obviously, Joan's problem did not seem to be informational. It was not that she wasn't convicted. It was that *desire* had not yet been heightened to the point of decision.

In this chapter I will introduce the basic tools for heightening desire. The application of these principles, as seen in the following conversation with Joan, will tremendously increase the number of positive decisions.

The pastor and I knocked at Joan's door one sunny afternoon. With a warm reception, she ushered us in to her living room. After being seat and having a brief, friendly talk, I spoke with confidence, "Joan, we are so delighted that for the last two years you've been able to attend the Adventist church and have enjoyed its fellowship. During this period of time there have been many Bible truths presented; no doubt, some have been new to you. Do you have any questions at all about the things that you've been learning?"

"No, I really don't," she replied.

"Joan, is it clear to you that Jesus Christ is soon to return to this world in power and great glory?"

"Why, yes, it is. Christ's coming is certainly the only hope for the world."

"Have you, as far as you know, accepted Jesus Christ as your Lord and Saviour?"

"Oh, yes, I have. In fact, even before I attended the Adventist Church I made a commitment to become a Christian."

"You've learned about the Bible Sabbath and the state of man in death, and healthful living. Do you have any questions about the distinct doctrines of the Adventist Church?"

"Well, no, I really don't. I believe these doctrines are true."

Now I knew for certain that her problem was not informational. Sensing that Joan had a very strong, close relationship with her family and that for her to make a decision to become a Seventh-day Adventist meant, in her mind, being separated from their love and support, I zeroed in on one of the *benefits* of being baptized and becoming part of the family of God. Once again, I used a Bible text. "Joan, there are some people who, as they think of being baptized, develop a real fear. They fear what they're going to lose. The Bible says in 2 Corinthians 6:17: 'Wherefore come out from among them, and be ye separate, saith the Lord.' And often that's all that's read. But the 17th and 18th verses say, 'And I will receive you. And will be a Father unto you, and ye shall be my sons and daughters, saith the Lord Almighty.'"

As I looked at Joan, I knew that the text appealed deeply to her heart, so I followed through with a comment something like this: "Joan, you might be thinking about the possibility of alienation from your father or mother as you make this decision. You may be thinking about losing friends. But I'd like you to picture in your mind Jesus with His arms outstretched, telling you that He will be a brother to you. His love is deeper than any earthly tie. You will become part of the royal line of the family of heaven. On earth you'll become part of a church that's a fellowship of brothers and sisters who love you. And Joan, I'd like to invite you to become a part of this kind of warm, loving fellowship."

As Joan saw, not what she was losing, but the benefit of what she was gaining, she made her decision to become part of the family of God by uniting with His Church.

Decisions are made, not simply as men and women are convicted of what they ought to do, but as they develop the desire to act on their conviction. Presenting information deepens conviction; desire is heightened as men and women see the *benefits* of taking the right action as contrasted with the *consequences* of taking the wrong action. Although our motive in serving God is not to receive benefits, there are definite rewards in serving Him, as well as consequences for not serving Him. The Bible is full of such benefits, which are actually appeals from Jesus offering us a more abundant life.

1. *The benefit of inner peace as opposed to inner turmoil.* Jesus says in John 14:27, "Peace I leave with you, my peace I give unto you: not as the world giveth, give I unto you. Let not your heart be troubled, neither let it be afraid." Ps. 119:165 adds, "Great peace have they which love thy law: and nothing shall offend them."

These texts do not mean that the lives of those who serve God are free from problems. To assure men and women of that is to be dishonest. But I can assure them that if they are convicted to do what is right and they ignore the leading of God, they will have no genuine inner peace. If, however, they are convicted of what God wants them to do and act on such convictions, they will receive an inner quality of peace in their relationship with Jesus Christ that cannot be attained in any other way. Now let us apply this.

Suppose a man agrees that the Bible Sabbath is indeed true, but is struggling over it because he has a Sabbath work problem. He's concerned about providing for his family. He's concerned about what friends will think if he makes this kind of decision. He's concerned about how his wife is going to react. In my appeal to this person I might say something like this:

"John, indeed you have a great deal to be concerned about in the decision that is confronting you. You are convicted that the Bible Sabbath is right, aren't you?"

"Yes, I am."

"John, we've talked, too, about the fact that the Sabbath is going to be the final test of inner loyalty and commitment in the last crisis. I know you want to be on God's side, don't you?"

Quietly he nods. I know the problem is neither information nor conviction. I move on to desire.

"Now, John, we've discussed three major problems that you are facing: The problem of your family's disapproval, the concern over what your friends might think, and the possibility you may lose your job. All these things are producing some conflict aren't they?"

"Sure are."

"John, might I read you two Bible texts?" And then I would read him John 16:33 and Psalm 119:65, appealing on this basis: "John, God is offering you something. He's offering inner peace. And I would rather do what I know to be right and have peace within and conflict without, than to have peace without and conflict within. You can walk away from the Bible truth regarding the Sabbath. It would resolve the problem of your Sabbath work and some of the conflict at home. It might even resolve some of the tension among your friends. But since you know what is right, it would not resolve this one thing—the terrible conflict within you. You would forfeit the peace that God wants to give you. John, why don't we kneel down and tell Christ that you want His peace dwelling in your heart, that peace is more important to you than anything in this world."

2. *The benefit of receiving the Holy Spirit.* In Acts 5:32, Peter shares God's promise, "We are his witnesses of these things; and so is also the Holy Ghost, whom God hath given to them that obey him." To whom is the Holy Ghost given? To those who *obey.*

In John 14:15 Jesus expands the thought, "If ye love me, keep my commandments. And I will pray the Father, and he shall give you another Comforter, that he may abide with you for ever." The Scriptures directly relate the reception of the Holy Spirit to obeying the commands of God. This appeal is especially effective for Pentecostal Christians. If I'm working with a Pentecostal couple, for example, my appeal on the topic of health might go something like this:

"John and Mary, you are able to see now that the principle of healthful living is one of the basic commands that Christ has given in Scripture. As you make this decision to give up pork because it's not in harmony with God's will, this commitment will enable you to be a greater open channel for the Holy Spirit, and He will fill you more fully than you have ever experienced before."

In making an appeal to a charismatic on the Sabbath, I might say, "You have desired to be a Spirit-filled Christian. The Bible says, 'If you love me, keep my commandments. And I will pray the Father, and he shall give you another Comforter, that may abide with you forever.' The Spirit does not fill some people to a greater degree and others to a lesser because of a partiality on the Spirit's part. But some people come with pint containers, some with quart, and some with gallon. Some come with swimming pools! The larger your commitment and the more complete your obedience, the more capable the Holy Spirit is of filling you. Now, John and Mary, you do want to be filled totally with the Holy Spirit, don't you? And as you keep the Sabbath because you love Jesus Christ, the Holy Spirit will have a greater capacity to fill."

3. *The benefit of true happiness.* John 13:17 says, "If ye know these things, happy are ye if ye do them." In John 10:10 Jesus adds, "I am come that they might have life, and that they might have it more abundantly." If I am talking to a young couple who love life in all of its fullness, I will look at them and say something like this:

"Peter, Sandy, as you look ahead in life with your three-year-old and your five-year-old, what you really desire, I am sure, is happiness. God indeed wants to give you a happy life. The reason that God has given you the message to stay away from alcohol, tobacco, and unclean foods, for example, is not because He wants to be a restrictive judge, but because He loves you. He doesn't want to see His precious children getting lung cancer. He wants you to be happy. He's given you the Sabbath so you won't have a nervous breakdown, so you can relax one day a week, so you can fellowship with Him, so you can spend time in the afternoons with your family in nature. He's given you the message about the state of man in death because He doesn't want you to be tormented about what happens to a person when he dies. He wants you to be happy. The Bible is a manual for happiness."

4. *The benefit of a heavenly home.* I will often describe heaven for certain individuals, drawing a contrast with the tawdry pleasures of this world. In Hebrews 11:24 the Bible says "By faith Moses when he was come to years, refused to be called the son of Pharaoh's daughter; Choosing rather to suffer affliction with the people of God, than to enjoy the pleasures of sin for a season; Esteeming the reproach of Christ greater riches than the treasures of Egypt: for he had respect unto the recompense of the reward."

Throughout the Bible, men and women of faith looked for eternity. Abraham looked for a city whose builder and maker was God. One of the great benefits of deciding for Jesus Christ and living in harmony with His truth is the hope of heaven at last. Think of the impact it might have on the life of a 28-year-old woman whose career is on the line if she works on the Bible Sabbath. A sensitive appeal for decision might go something like this:

"Let's talk about a thousand years from now, or maybe ten thousand years from now, or a million years from now. What would you really like to be doing a million years from now?"

She smiles and swallows hard. The appeal continues. "Picture this scene: fields of waving grain, green hillsides, flowers dotting the landscape with red and yellow and blue. Crystal clear ponds, deep blue sky. Fruits of every size and shape. Everything to delight the eye and satisfy the taste. A land where there's no sickness, no sorrow, no death, where every inhabitant is filled with life and joy, where love emanates from every being. A land where you can build your own house and inhabit it and eat the fruit of your gardens. A place where every talent is developed, every capacity expanded. A place where you can travel from world to world, from star to star.

"Now, Mary, is anything worth missing that world? Think of meeting Jesus Christ, Himself, and watching as He stretches out His nail-scarred hand and says to you, 'All of this is for you—I died to make it possible.' If you compare this with what you'd have to give up now to serve Him, is there any comparison? I know God is going to help you make that decision today and to look forward to Bible baptism in the light of the beauty of heaven." Our appeal here is to get the eyes of the person off the problems being faced on earth, and onto heavenly realities; to show clearly the contrast between what he/she is clinging to and what all of heaven has to offer.

5. *The benefit of forgiveness of sin and freedom from guilt.* This appeal especially encourages baptism. It can be based on Acts 2:37-39: "Now when they heard this, they were pricked in their hearts, and said unto Peter and to the rest of the apostles, Men and brethren, what shall we do? Then Peter said unto them, Repent, and be baptized every one of you in the name of Jesus Christ for the remission of sins, and ye shall receive the gift of the Holy Ghost. For the promise is unto you, and to your children, and to all that are afar off, even as many as the Lord our God shall call."

Acts 22:16 asks, "And now why tarriest thou? arise, and be baptized, and wash away thy sins, calling on the name of the Lord." Baptism symbolizes cleansing from sin. A powerful incentive for baptism is a sense of freedom from guilt.

Just a few years ago a couple came to my evangelistic meetings whose lives had been badly bruised by sin. The husband had been a heavy drinker, and both he and his wife were on their second marriage. The guilt of their past haunted them like an ugly monster. As they thought about Bible baptism as a symbol of cleansing from the guilt of the past, they realized they would stand before God as if they had never sinned. They saw the benefit of freedom from guilt, and longed for baptism. For two weeks they kept saying, "Pastor, can't we be baptized this Sabbath?"

In his book, *The Mind Changers,* Griffith describes the principal benefits people derive from change by using the psychological term "minimax." Students of human behavior have concluded that minimax is the main motivating factor in human behavior. It declares that individuals will act on a given item when the benefits are maximum and the risk minimum—minimax. Maximizing the eternal benefits of right action will produce dramatically greater results than focusing on the negative consequences of that action.

It was discovered that one group of dock workers in San Francisco unloaded twice as much cargo in half the time with less breakage. Researchers were eager to discover why. As they probed, they found that each group had "dollies" available, but only the most efficient group used them. Even the word "dolly" is repulsive to rough, burly dockmen. Most foremen attempted to motivate their crews by such expressions as "The rules say you have to use the dolly. Use it or you may get fired!" The foreman who motivated his crew most successfully presented benefits. He often shouted, "Save your back, stupid, use the cart!" In effect, his message was interpreted: "The smart guys have healthy backs because they use the dolly." This same principle of emphasizing benefits applies to spiritual things, as well.

Jesus' example provides a model in positively motivating people. You will recall Peter came to Jesus saying, "Lo, we have left all, and have followed thee." (Mark 10:28). The implication is clear, Peter's real question was, "Lord we have given up so much, what will we receive in return?" Jesus answer is a classic. It shows how He motivated people.

> ... *No one who has left house or brothers or sisters or father or mother or wife or children or lands for my sake or the gospels who will not receive a hundred-fold now in this time, houses and brothers and sisters and mothers and children and lands, with persecutions, and in the age to come eternal life.*
>
> —Mark 10:29,30, RSV

Jesus' words are too plain to be misunderstood. Whatever an individual gives up Jesus offers a thousand times more in return—His peace, His spiritual power to overcome sin, the joy of fellowship with other Christians, the inner happiness in knowing we are doing God's will—all of these are immeasurable blessings.

All through the gospel Jesus offers the amazing benefits of following Him. Ask the Lord to help you share the right benefit with the right person. Ask the Holy Spirit to help you know who needs what benefit and watch your number of decisions increase.

Continuing Education Assignment

1. List the names of two persons you are presently leading to a spiritual decision:

    Name:
    What benefit(s) would most appeal to him/her?
    What texts would work best in presenting this benefit?

2. Define the minimax principle.

5

The Motivation:
Negative and Positive Motivators

Listening to Jonathan Edwards' noted sermon, "Sinners in the Hands of An Angry God," his congregation could almost feel the flames of hell, and as the wrath of God poured hotter and hotter from the pulpit, it was a rare soul who did not surrender his all to serve God. Looking at such an extreme example of fear as a motivation for Christian service, one could almost conclude that such negative emotion has no part in bringing men and women to Christ. Is there ever a valid use of fear as a motivating factor in character change?

Fear Can Distort

Certainly Edwards presented a distorted picture of the character of God, and vastly abused the fear factor. Each of us would agree that if fear is the prime motive for moving men and women to decision, then something is seriously wrong.

On the other hand, the Word of God does clearly portray the contrasting destinies of heaven and hell as eternal rewards for men and women who accept or reject Christ. Heaven provides motivation for being saved, and hell a deterrent from being lost. The fear of hell may keep men and women from doing things that they otherwise would do, and thus provide an impetus for leading people to the Saviour. Fear, then, can have a positive influence in a person's life, provided it does not become so overwhelming that it blocks and distorts the balanced message of the gospel.

Fear Can Motivate

Even in everyday living fear serves as a protection. Fear keeps a child from burning his hand on the stove. Fear keeps a small boy from running out into the street after a ball. Fear causes me to check for my driver's license when I get into my car, so that I won't be arrested. Fear is a legitimate motive, but it's not the whole picture. Fear may provide the catalyst, the temporary call for action, but it will never alone bring about a deep and solid conviction.

Throughout the Bible Christ Himself uses the motive of fear in prompting men and women to serve Him. In the parable of the wheat and the tares, He focuses on two classes of people at the end of time. The parables of the sheep and the goats, and the net with the discarded fish illustrate the two ways to live—one leading to eternal life and the other to final destruction. In one of His most moving appeals, Jesus climaxes a sermon in Matthew 16: "For what is a man profited, if he shall gain the whole world, and lose his own soul? or what shall a man give in exchange for his soul?" In Matthew 25:46, He once again points to the destiny of all mankind: "And these shall go away into everlasting punishment: but the righteous into life eternal."

Spiritual decisions are so significant because eternity lasts so long. If I am struggling with a soul to make a decision for Christ, I might say something like this:

"Eternity is a long time, John and Mary, and God has given you and me the capacity to choose how we will spend it. He says, 'Now is the accepted time; behold, now is the day of salvation." 2 Cor. 6:2. Joshua says in chapter 24:15, 'Choose you this day whom ye will serve; . . . but as for me and my house, we will serve the Lord.' Christ invites you to decide tonight to go all the way with Him. He will never let you down. He will take you from here to eternity. As you consider heaven and hell, remember that your choice makes all the difference. God will not coerce. He says, 'My child, here are the two: the joy of heaven, and the agony of hell.' Think of what it would be like to be lost; to be separated from God, your friends, your husband, your wife, your children. Think of what it would be like to be in outer darkness, where the Bible says there will be weeping and gnashing of teeth. John and Mary, with eternity in heaven before you, with hell behind you, motivated by the Christ you love, why not just tell Jesus tonight as we kneel, 'Dear Lord, I do want to spend eternity with you, and I want to seal my acceptance of You and Your truth by being baptized this coming Sabbath.'"

We Fear Present Loss

A strong appeal can be based on the *eternal* consequences of sin. It is also effective to point to the negative consequences in this *present* life as a result of continued persistence in wrongdoing. Some time ago I was counseling with a man who was a heavy drinker. As I spoke to him of the love and mercy of Christ, I could see that nothing I said was reaching him. Realizing that no progress could be made until this man faced the implications of his present lifestyle, I took a turn in my appeal.

Facing him honestly, I asked, "Can you see that you are very close to losing most of your money, your self-esteem, your stability in life? If you continue drinking, it will lead you to financial ruin and deep debt. Your marriage is already in trouble. How much more pressure can it take? How will it feel to be without money, without a job, without a wife, without even a roof over your head? And after that, what? After life is over, will you be without heaven too?" Such a clear revelation of the facts startled this man so much that he was able to begin the process of change.

Specific Consequences of Wrongdoing

The consequences of wrong doing are paraded before us in the Bible. Committing a few of these texts to memory can be a great asset in enabling us to show both the benefits of right and the consequences of wrong action.

A failure to respond to truth and do what I know in my heart to be right leads to the following consequences:

1. *Removal of further light.* John 12:35 says, "Walk while ye have the light, lest darkness come upon you: for he that walketh in darkness knoweth not whither he goeth."

2. *Acceptance of lies.* In 2 Thess. 2:8-12, the Bible clearly points out that those who receive not the love of the truth that they might be saved, will be sent a strong delusion that they shall believe a lie.

3. *Rejecting the Holy Spirit.* Only the Spirit can lead us into all truth (John 16:13; John 14:15, 16).

With these consequences in mind, one might appeal for decision on this basis: "Peter and Joan, you've sensed the convicting power of God, having seen clearly the truth revealed in His Word. The Bible says, 'Walk while ye have the light, lest darkness come upon you.' It's dangerous not to accept the truth. God says that once truth has been revealed, those who don't accept it will ultimately believe a lie. And the Bible tells us that many who choose not to receive the love of the truth will, in turn, reject the Holy Spirit. You don't want the darkness and the lies of Satan and the rejection of the Holy Spirit. Would it not be well for us tonight to tell Jesus, 'Lord, since I'm convicted that these things are true, I want You to give me strength and power to walk in them.'"

Ellen White stated it succinctly when she said, "Few believe with heart and soul that we have a hell to shun and a heaven to win" (*Desire of Ages,* p. 636). Soul winners are deeply conscious of the fact that they present before their hearers two pathways—the way of eternal life and the way of eternal death. Men and women are either saved or lost! It is either heaven or hell! It is either salvation or damnation! The Bible says that hell is a place of eternal separation, a place without the slightest hope. (Matt. 8:12, Luke 13:28, Matt. 25:46, Heb. 6:2). Although Seventh-day Adventists categorically reject the unbiblical concept of an ever-burning hell, we definitely recognize that eternity is forever! And the fear of eternal loss is a legitimate motive in prompting desire.

When I was a fifth-grade student attending a Catholic parochial school, a nun used an illustration that has influenced my thinking throughout the years. One of the students asked, "Sister, how long is eternity?"

The nun responded, "Children, picture the ocean." I was brought up on the New England sea coast, and my young mind easily pictured the wide expanse of an endless ocean with whitecapped waves breaking upon the shore.

She continued, "Picture a sea gull, a sea gull which would come once every thousand years to take a single drop out of the ocean. When the sea gull has drained the ocean dry, that would be the first second of eternity."

My little fifth-grade mind began to understand eternity is a long, long, long, long time!

Indeed it is. And men and women who are confronted with the claims of the cross must understand that Christ's death enables them to live with Him in heaven forever. But to reject that death means that forever they will be lost. Present before your hearers the two ways, and watch your results increase.

Evangelistic meetings or evangelistic visits that are couched in a laissez-faire, take-it-or-leave-it attitude will produce little conviction and motivate little desire. Use texts in your preaching and visiting that illustrate the benefits of right doing, but also clarify the consequences of wrong doing, and they will be a strong tool in prompting an individual to make a full commitment to right.

One of the things we have discovered in our evangelistic meetings is that the meeting produces conviction, but it is the responsibility of the visitor to deepen that conviction so that it may lead to a desire for change. Texts which clarify the consequences of wrongdoing can be a strong tool in prompting an individual to make a full commitment to right.

Continuing Education Assignment

1. Under what circumstances would you feel the use of fear is appropriate in calling for spiritual decisions?

2. Under what circumstances is it inappropriate?

3. How did Jesus use fear?

4. What specific consequences have resulted from your using fear in asking people to decide for Christ?

5. Have you used it too little? too much?

6

The Impact:
Importance of Influence

Tom lived in a luxurious suburb and held a top managerial position in a prestigious corporation. Everything about him reflected success: his dress was meticulous, his home beautiful, his children bright and attractive. And Tom presided over it all with a demeanor demanding respect. His organizational and executive skills were balanced with an unassuming nature, a gentle, communicative temperament. His wife and children deeply admired him.

Years before he had been educated in Adventist schools. Now he had attended our meetings and was convicted of the truth, but he feared that religion would bring unrealistic demands on his current lifestyle. For weeks Tom had difficulty making a decision to be baptized. As I prayed and searched for some possible way to help him, I began to realize that a traditional approach of "promised riches" held out no appeal for this man who felt secure in his current situation. "Benefits" and "consequence"' would have little compelling power with Tom. I was left with the word "expectations." As I thought about it, the *expectations of others* would likely be the issue which would prompt Tom to action. He was a man looked up to, admired, and followed. And his influence upon others was something which he did not take lightly.

As we sat together in his lush den, my appeal went something like this: "Tom, as you've been coming to the meetings, have any questions come up concerning doctrines you have heard there?"

I already knew that most things were clear to him, but I asked the question for two reasons. First, to clear away any major obstacles which might possibly exist; but, more importantly, to give him the opportunity to express his confidence, since I was quite sure he was in agreement with everything that had been presented. Once Tom, himself, had established the fact of his agreement with our teachings, he would be in a better position to consider seriously the appeal to follow.

He nodded in assent, "Yes, I have believed the tenets of the Adventist faith for some time."

"Tom, as I was thinking of you the other day, I thought of what an influential man you are and the tremendous impact your life has upon others. I saw how your wife admires you. I noted the look of pleasure in her eyes as she watched you turn the pages of your Bible. I noticed how your little son and daughter look up to you. I know that the decision you're considering is a very weighty one, that you are the kind of man who considers his actions and decisions seriously before making them. But Tom, I know that if you make a decision to be baptized it will thrill your wife and direct your children toward a life rich with Christian meaning and joy.

"There's many a man who comes to this type of decision and turns back, fearing the cost will be too high. Some do not have the courage to follow their convictions on issues such as Sabbath-keeping, tithe-paying, or abstinence from alcohol. But years later, the results of silencing that still, small voice become apparent. There is no moral standard in the home. Children follow any notion of popularity, ruining their lives with drugs, poor associations, and wrong choices. And all because there has been no guide to follow, no pattern of right held out before them. And, oh, the feelings of guilt that come to the father who knew the standard, but had not the courage to grasp the banner and hold it high.

"Tom, as you consider this decision for Christ, remember the words of Romans 14:7, that "none of us liveth to himself, and no man dieth to himself." Your children are young enough to watch your influence, to follow you in your commitment to Christ. There can be a path leading from your baptismal pool that they can follow all the way to eternity. If you become the spiritual leader in the family, you will be the model they will follow. If you will lead out in family worship, studying the Sabbath School lesson, getting up to go to church and Sabbath School, these children, I know, will follow you, and so will your wife. Tom, you have a tremendous responsibility on your job, but you have a greater responsibility as a spiritual leader in your home. For your wife's sake, for your children's sake—because you really want to lead them—would you like to tell Jesus Christ right now that you will look forward to baptism this coming Sabbath?"

As I made this appeal, we knelt there and Tom sealed his decision to totally commit his life to Christ in baptism. Tom's great need was to sense that the significance of his decision extended beyond the borders of his own existence, reaching into the lives of his wife and children. So do not underestimate the value, particularly to those of strong influence and character, of appealing to them on the basis of other lives they will touch. In every parent's heart God has put the desire to see their children live a meaningful and fulfilling life. It can be a powerful force in leading men and women to make a commitment to Christ.

As they spun the wheel of fortune, the old carnival barkers used to say, "'round and 'round she goes, and where she stops, nobody knows." There is a sense in which this is true of Christian witness, for we never know where the effects of a decision for Christ will end. The decision of a father, as we have seen, can affect his children. The decision of a wife can affect her husband. Often, if an individual delays making a decision for Christ until family or friends make a decision, it inhibits the others from making it.

My father made a decision to follow Jesus Christ and the truths of the Advent message years before my mother. It was that decision and his positive example that ultimately led our entire family to know the saving claims of Christ and the truth of the Advent message.

Some time ago a young woman counseled with me about the fact that her husband was not a Christian. My response to her was that her great responsibility was not to pressure, urge, or cajole, but to live Christ. Nevertheless, she should not wait for his decision. Her decision would have a powerful influence upon him.

Ultimately, through the influence of that woman, her husband accepted Christ, as did both of her children, her sister, her sister's boyfriend, her husband's brother, his wife and their entire family. As the result of this one woman's influence, more than ten have now accepted Jesus, the message of Adventism, and have been baptized. And the circle of influence goes on and on and on.

The Pyramiding Effect

One of the most amazing examples of the pyramiding effects of faith is told by James H. Sample in a 1967 article in *Christianity Today* entitled "Passing the Torch of Evangelism." This article says that when Moody was seventeen years old he went to Boston to work with his uncle who owned a shoe store. The uncle encouraged him to attend church, and Edward Kimball became his Sunday school teacher.

One day Kimball paid young Moody a visit at the store. Between customers, while the youth was putting away shoes in the back room, Kimball convinced Dwight Moody to give his life to Christ.

Years later, when he was preaching in England, Moody told the story of Kimball in the church of F. B. Meyer. Meyer's ministry was revolutionized—so was that of another young minister who heard Meyer speak at Moody's school in Northfield, Massachusetts. Meyer preached a powerful sermon on the willingness to surrender all to Christ. A young man sitting in the back row was transformed. His name was J. Wilber Chapman.

Chapman became a powerful evangelist and one of the most influential churchmen of his time. He had a great influence on a professional baseball player and Y.M.C.A. clerk by the name of Billy Sunday. Billy Sunday became known nationally for his evangelistic preaching.

Through Sunday's preaching in Charlotte, North Carolina, a layman's group was founded to witness for Christ in the community. In 1932 they organized a crusade and called Mordecai Hamm to preach. Hamm's preaching was disturbing to one sixteen-year-old high school senior who sat in the tent night after night. He and his friend thought they could escape by sitting behind the preacher in the choir. But such was not the case. Finally, young Billy Graham and his friend, Grady Wilson, accepted Christ.

The torch of influence passed from Kimball to Moody, from Moody to Meyer, from Meyer to Chapman, from Chapman to Sunday, from Sunday to Graham and Grady. Minor events, yet with significant major consequences. You will motivate men and women to make decisions for Jesus Christ as they see the influence of their decisions upon others. Help them to see how their decision is like a pebble thrown into a pond with ripples that go out from the shores of earth to the shores of eternity.

Ellen White's statement is directly to the point:

> *Every act of our lives affects others for good or evil. Our influence is tending upward or downward; it is felt, acted upon, and to a greater or less degree reproduced by others. If by our example we aid others in the development of good principles, we give them power to do good. In their turn they exert the same beneficial influence upon others, and thus hundreds and thousands are affected by our unconscious influence.*
> —*Testimonies for the Church*, vol. 2, p. 133

We've seen up to this point that yielding the will to Christ comes as the result of a number of factors. The initial level, ***infor-***

mation, provides a base from which *conviction* springs. However, only when an individual has developed a strong personal *desire* to follow those convictions does positive *action* come. Traditionally, Seventh-day Adventist training has stressed the importance of bringing people to conviction. Yet the art of motivating desire has been neglected.

For three chapters we've discussed how to awaken desire. It can be done by presenting the benefits of right doing, the consequences of wrong choices, or the expectations of others, such as family and friends. One last principle remains which will serve as the protoplasm of the evangelistic model, holding in place and giving life to all other principles thus presented as "The Significant Other."

Continuing Education Assignment

1. With what kinds of people would the principle of *expectations* work most effectively?

    Least effectively?

2. List names of those you are working with or have worked with who would be most persuaded by this principle.

3. The conclusion of this chapter summarizes what the book has attempted to teach thus far:

    a. The three prerequisites to action are:

    b. Desire can be awakened by appeals centered on what three areas?

7

The Attraction:
Jesus—the Significant Other

Kembleton Wiggins, in his book, *Soul Winning Made Easier*, discusses what he calls *cognitive consistency*. This principle asserts that when presented with a new idea, an individual attempts to find some type of consistency with his existing beliefs before integrating the new concept into his life. Thus, many people tend to resist change since it produces a tension of ideas. When new desires are awakened, however, a greater tension may be felt if one resists a change that he knows he ought to make. It is at this point, when men and women sense that *to do nothing* will conflict with their conscience, that desire results in action.

Christianity and Cognitive Consistency

When hearing the message of the seventh-day Sabbath, for example, individuals may experience some tension when considering a change of lifestyle. But if they have committed their lives totally to Jesus, and can sense the strong connection between keeping the Sabbath and showing their love for Christ, then they will experience a greater friction if they resist the Sabbath message. Therefore, to minimize the friction between themselves and Jesus, it would be easier for them to accept the Sabbath than to reject it.

Thus, there are three steps in cognitive consistency: (1) develop a deep love for Jesus in the hearts of those you are studying with, (2) present each testing truth as being very important to Jesus, emphasizing that Jesus expects them to accept and act upon the truth, and (3) show them that to resist the truth is not to resist the doctrine, but is actually to resist Jesus, the Author of that doctrine. It is one thing for individuals to reject the Sabbath as a doctrine; it is another thing for them to reject Christ as the Creator. It is one thing for people to resist healthful living as a doctrine; it is quite another thing for them to resist Jesus as the One who desires, by His Holy Spirit, to dwell in a clean body.

Let us suppose an individual resist giving up unclean foods and I go to visit. I can read all the proof texts illustrating God's desire for him/her to stop eating unclean foods, but probably the person is already convicted on the issue; that is the reason for the struggle. Acceptance of the Bible injunction calls for a radical change in a pattern established over years of sitting down at the table. This produces friction. It is my job, as I visit, to help release that friction. And so I might make an appeal something like this:

"John, suppose Jesus were here tonight and said to you, 'Do you love Me?' I know you'd say, 'Oh, Lord, I love you deeply.' Then suppose Jesus said, 'Do you love me enough to give up unclean foods for me?' If Jesus Christ were here Himself and asked you, what would you say?"

John's response is immediate. "Why, there would be no question. I would tell Him yes, I'd give up anything He asked me to."

I continue, "Listen to Him speak to you when He says in 1 Corinthians 3:17, 'If any man defile the temple of God, him shall God destroy.' Listen to Him as He calls for your complete commitment in 1 Corinthians 10:31, 'Whether therefore ye eat, or drink, or whatsoever ye do, do all to the glory of God.' Listen to His personal message in 1 Corinthians 6:19 and 20, 'What? know ye not that your body is the temple of the Holy Ghost which is in you, which ye have of God, and ye are not your own? For ye are bought with a price: therefore glorify God in your body, and in your spirit, which are God's.'

"These texts are Jesus, Himself, talking to you. He's using the Bible to communicate an important message from heaven to you. Won't you tell Him, 'Dear Jesus, since You personally have invited me to give up unclean foods and because I love You, I desire to do it?"

The apostle Paul clearly illuminated this principle in his own life's experience. He states:

> *But whatever former things I had that might have been gains to me, I have come to consider as (one combined) loss for Christ's sake. Yes, furthermore I count everything as loss compared to the possession of the priceless privilege—the overwhelming preciousness, the surpassing worth and supreme advantage—of knowing Christ Jesus my Lord, and of progressively becoming more deeply and intimately acquainted with Him, of perceiving and recognizing and understanding Him more fully and clearly. For His sake I have lost everything and consider it all to be mere rubbish (refuse, dregs), in order that I may win (gain) Christ, the Anointed One.*
>
> —Phil. 3:7, 8, *Amplified*

The major motivating factor enabling men and women to make decisions is the fact that Jesus Christ left heaven, tabernacled in human flesh, lived a perfect life, and was nailed to a cross in an act of supreme love. It is the Christ of the cross that attracts. He breaks the hold of sin.

Jesus Himself, said, "And I, if I be lifted up from the earth, will draw all men unto me" (John 12:32). Ellen White adds,

The very first and most important thing is to melt and subdue the soul by presenting our Lord Jesus Christ as the sin-pardoning Saviour"
—Testimonies for the Church, volume 6, pp. 53, 54

She also adds,

The wonderful love of Christ will melt and subdue hearts when the mere reiteration of doctrines would accomplish nothing."
—The Desire of Ages, p. 826

The gospel transforms lives. Recently in Moscow a man in his mid-twenties burst into the room I was resting in between two evangelistic meetings. Initially I thought he was going to attack me. He appeared out of control. When my translator finally got him calmed down, we discovered the young bearded man before us was one of Moscow's notorious criminals. He had been in and out of court more than twenty times. But now he was so burdened with guilt, he begged for help. He desired immediate release from the guilt that was destroying his life. Once again I simply presented the gospel. Accepting Christ, he fell to his knees sobbing, a great peace came over him. Today he is a faithful Adventist Christian singing in the Moscow Adventist Choir.

Dr. S. D. Gordon tells of an old Christian woman whose age began to affect her memory. She had once known much of the Bible by heart. Eventually only one precious bit stayed with her, "I know whom I have believed and am persuaded that he is able to keep that which I have committed unto him against that day." By and by, part of that slipped away, and she would quietly repeat, "that which I've committed unto him."

At last, as she hovered on the borderline between this and the eternal world, her loved ones noticed her lips moving. They bent down to see if she needed anything. She was repeating over and over again to herself the one word of the text that she remembered "Him, Him, Him." She had lost her whole Bible, but one word captured her attention. One word inspired her with hope, and in that one word she understood the most significant truth of the Bible—that Christ is all in all.

Jesus Is the Significant Other

The appeal to consider Jesus as the Significant Other adds powerful motivation to any doctrine presented. One may feel pressured because his neighbor wants him to do one thing, his boss another, and his wife yet another. But Jesus is the Significant Other. He is the One whose plea outweighs anyone else's. And when a person vacillates between pleasing others and following the truth of the Scriptures, friction will be released only when Jesus is seen as the most important person in life. Appealing on this basis, I might ask: "Mary, who is the most significant person in your life? Is it your father or mother? Your sister or brother? Your husband or a friend? Who means more to you than anyone else in the world?" Before Mary can even respond, I insert, "How do you weigh their counsel as it compares to Christ's?"

Almost always, a person will quickly respond, "Oh, the most significant person in my life is Jesus Christ."

The appeal can then continue: "If indeed He is, will you not follow Him as He invites you to keep the Sabbath? He says, 'If you love me, keep my commandments.' Will you show Him your total commitment? Jesus, the most significant person in your life, invites you to express this by taking the step of baptism."

In this appeal, Jesus Christ, the Significant Other, is the One who is totally exalted as the basis of all decision. This emphasis is especially effective with people who have been converted Christians for a number of years—people who have walked with Christ, listened to His voice, and studied the Bible to determine His will. An appeal to do what Jesus requests cannot be ignored by those who consider Him to be the Significant Other in their lives.

The soul winner's work is similar to that of the receptionist in the doctor's waiting room. Her goal is not to operate on diseased people. It is, rather, to get them to the doctor, who has the knowledge, skill, and understanding to perform the operation. It is her job to introduce them to him. Thus, in all soul-winning work our goal is to lead people to Jesus, to show them what He wants them to do, not what we desire. It is to help them make Christ's will supreme in their lives, and thus choose His will rather than their own. It is to help them make Christ the Significant Other so that the authority of His influence is greater than any other influence on earth.

Continuing Education Assignment

1. Define "cognitive consistency."

2. List the three steps in cognitive consistency.

3. Take out a typical Bible study or evangelistic sermon you have prepared on a uniquely Seventh-day Adventist doctrine such as the Sabbath, state of the dead, etc. Write out an evaluation of how well it follows the three steps above.

8

The Process:
The Clear and Set Principle

Ed was obviously troubled. I had made a statement in a sermon that conflicted with his understanding of Scripture. He didn't question a major doctrine such as the manner of Christ' coming, the Sabbath, the state of the dead, or the health message. He was bothered by a little point that I'd made regarding Judas. While preaching on the divinity of Christ and the crucifixion scene, I casually mentioned that after Judas betrayed Jesus he hanged himself, the rope snapped, and he landed on the rocks below, dead.

After the meeting Ed pushed to the front of the auditorium, full of questions. "Where does the Bible say Judas fell down? How could you make a definitive statement like that with no Bible evidence?" Before the next meeting, we spent fifteen minutes discussing Ed's question. It was only as I read Acts 1:18 that the expression on Ed's face began to change. He listened with obvious surprise to the words, "Now this man purchased a field with the reward of iniquity; and falling headlong, he burst asunder in the midst, and all his bowels gushed out." Quite a gory story, but Ed's confidence in the solid Bible basis for our meetings was reaffirmed.

Later that evening, as I made an appeal for men and women to surrender their lives fully to Christ, I was thrilled to see that Ed was one of the first to stand. I had learned a basic principle in how people make decisions.

The human mind is so constructed that if even one minor point cannot be reconciled with existing ideas, confidence is destroyed in the carrier of that information. It was a minor point that entered Ed's mind, yet, unless it was cleared up, his confidence in me would have been undermined. This means that the one who presents a series of Bible doctrines, and hopes to "clear everything up" with some sort of grand finale, ought to be prepared to lose a number of interests along the way. For if unanswered questions begin to accumulate in the mind, individuals may lose interest in a Bible study or evangelistic series, sealing themselves off from the person presenting those conflicting ideas. Therefore, it is absolutely vital to deal with each issue as it arises regardless of its apparent insignificance.

Truth Is Progressive

The "clear and set" principle teaches that only as new truths are clarified and confirmed in the minds of the listeners can future truths be received and accepted. The presenter must ascertain, at every new step, whether the hearers accept or reject the message, and how they have decided to integrate these new concepts into their present value structure. If this is not done, resistance will continue to build to the point of rejection. Truth is progressive.

The book of Proverbs states the maxim this way: "But the path of the just is as the shining light, that shineth more and more unto the perfect day" (Prov. 4:18). The principle is eternal: God allows light to shine more and more brightly along the pathway of individuals as truth is received and accepted. Any truths which appear hazy or inconsistent provide obstacles for further progress, but clearly-understood truths become stepping stones for further understanding of God's Word.

Ellen White emphasizes the "clear and setting" process of progressive decision throughout her writings. She says:

> *The sacred responsibility rests upon the minister to watch for souls as one that must give an account. He must interest himself in the souls for whom he labors, finding out all that perplexes and troubles them, and hinders them from walking in the light of the truth.*
> —*Review and Herald*, August 30, 1892.

If you do not know what hinders individuals from keeping the Sabbath, you may visit them ten times and get nowhere. Your efforts to win them are like beating the air. Unless you deal with the objections they face on that subject, you will be powerless in bringing them to a decision. Future subjects will be more cloudy and difficult, and additional ideas that bombard their minds and conflict with what they previously believed will ultimately lead to total rejection. The better the worker is able to discover what hinders individuals from deciding, and to clear them on that which is already presented, the more successful a soul winner he/she will be.

Ellen White again focuses upon the "clear and set" principle:

> *Many a laborer fails in his work because he does not come close to those who most need his help. With the Bible in hand, he should seek in a courteous manner to learn the objections which exist in the minds of those who are beginning to inquire, "What is truth?" Carefully and tenderly should he lead and educate them, as pupils in a school.*
> —*Gospel Workers* p. 190

Jesus reached souls because He was acquainted with their problems. His teachings were adapted to their situation. He understood the objection in their minds.

Mrs. White further states:

> *The minister must know the nature of the difficulties in the minds of the people that he may know how to give every man his portion in due season.* —Manuscript 4, 1893

Diagnostic Questions

The art of asking diagnostic questions is essential in discovering and dealing with objections that may arise. In visiting individuals who have just heard a Bible presentation on the second coming of Christ, I might seek to uncover any uncertainty or objection by engaging in a discussion such as this:

"John, Mary, we have been so delighted that you have been able to attend the Bible lectures for the last few weeks. How did you folks happen to learn about our seminar?"

Gaining from this a little *background* about the couple, I might then casually ask, "Are you enjoying the meetings?" This helps me assess their basic *attitude* toward what they are hearing. Next, I might question if John and Mary have been able to make it to each meeting up to that point. Although I generally know the *pattern of attendance*, I raise such a question to discover what specifically might be the cause of missed meetings. If someone says, "Oh, I can't come on Wednesday night because I have a Bible class which I attend," or "I can't come on Friday night because I work," I have gained a little more information which may prove helpful later on.

Next, I make a transition in the discussion which leads to an *affirming statement* on their part. "You've noticed we propose to present everything directly from the Bible at our seminar. Have you felt that everything presented is right from the Bible?"

Once some type of affirmation has been made, I become more specific in my discussion, opening up the conversation for any *objections* that John and Mary may be having. "Just the other night we discussed the subject of how Christ will return. Have you always understood what the Bible teaches regarding the second coming of Christ?" This is where clarification becomes important. If John and Mary have questions on the subject of the tribulation and the rapture, for example, it's time to work over the texts with them in their home.

If there is no objection at this point, it is good to close with a call for *commitment.* "It's a thrilling thing to know that Christ is coming and very soon," I might begin. "I know deep in my heart, that I want to be ready. I look forward to being in that group that will say, 'Lo, this is our God, we have waited for Him, and He will save us.' John and Mary, would you like to kneel together with me tonight as I pray that God will give us the strength to walk in the truth outlined in His Word, so that through His grace we will be ready to meet Him when He comes?"

Leaving the home, I know that I have accomplished two things concerning the second coming. First, I have discovered whether John and Mary have accepted this truth. And second, I have invited them to make a commitment to follow it—"clear and set."

In dealing with the Sabbath, I do not look for such a commitment after my initial presentation. Since this topic is often very new, and acceptance of it may involve serious changes in one's job or current lifestyle, I allow more time for the Holy Spirit to work, saving my appeal until after a second presentation.

At that later visit I ask three specific questions. It is important to note, at this point, that such questions do not come as a barrage of memorized inquiries uttered immediately upon entering a home. The questions which follow are effective only when given in the security of a warm relationship already established through open and sensitive communication. This is true both in an evangelistic series and a home Bible study.

1. *Previous Exposures:* "Have you folks ever heard a message on the Bible Sabbath before, or is the Sabbath new to you?" People often come back with unexpected responses. "Oh, in Sunday School years ago I always wondered why we kept the first day when the commandment said the seventh day was the Sabbath." Another might respond, "I had a book called *Bible Readings for the Home Circle,* which discussed the Bible Sabbath." Or, "My grandfather was an Adventist and he believed the Sabbath." It's equally important when someone answers, "No, I've never heard anything about the Sabbath before."

2. *Understanding:* "Do you have any questions about the Bible Sabbath, or is the Sabbath clear to you?" Often an individual will bring up honest concerns involving his job commitments, or family and friends. The person may be wondering about the status of loved ones who have attended church on Sunday for fifty years

before they died. This is where it is important to spend quality time in the home, gently but effectively dealing with each issue as it arises. Thousands have found my little book *Studying Together* a helpful tool in answering the objections people bring up.

3. *Commitment:* "Have you yet begun to think about keeping the Bible Sabbath?" If the response is positive, I encourage them to keep the Sabbath immediately. If the response is not positive, I close with, "I know if Jesus were here today and He asked you to keep the Bible Sabbath, you would be willing to do it, because you want to please Jesus, don't you? Let's just kneel down and ask Him to show you from His Word what He wants you to do. John, Mary, I know these things are new to you, but if the Word of God says them and Jesus teaches them, I know you want to follow. So let's pray and tell Jesus that today. Would you like to do that?"

Closing with prayer, I shake John and Mary's hands, telling them how thankful I am that they're willing to follow the truth, and urging them to continue coming to the meetings. Before leaving I provide them with my book on the Sabbath entitled the *Almost Forgotten Day*.

Thus, through the effective use of three diagnostic questions, I have discovered their previous exposure to the Sabbath, answered existing objections, and begun to "clear" John and Mary on the issue before a new topic is presented. Basically this is the process of progressive decision.

Seven Major Decisions

The above questioning and dialogue should take place as you work with an individual through each of the seven major decisions one must make to become a Seventh-day Adventist. "Clearing points" include acceptance of and commitment to the following:

1. The *inspiration of the Bible* and its revelation of *Jesus Christ* as the divine Savior of the world.

2. The special message of Christ to prepare people to meet Him at His *second coming*.

3. Christ's call for full obedience to His *law,* including the Bible *Sabbath.*

4. God's plea to *respect our bodies* as the temple of God, and to give up alcohol, tobacco, and unclean foods.

5. The Bible teaching of the *state of man in death*, in contrast to the rising view of spiritualism in the world.

6. The Bible and the *gift of prophecy* as identifying marks of the remnant church, and a desire to live up to the standards of

both.

7. *Baptism* as the sign and seal of accepting Christ, and becoming a part of His church on earth.

As the Holy Spirit leads men and women to accept each major doctrine, they develop more and more each day "unto the measure of the stature of the fullness of Christ." The process of leading people to Jesus is not one in which we hand them a large package at the end of a series, labeled "The Entire Message." Such a package would be too heavy, too complex, and too difficult to accept all at once. Rather, the effective process of soul winning offers small packages as the studies progress. Learners experience an understanding and acceptance of each new subject before the next one is offered—"clear and set."

Continuing Education Assignment

1. Define the term "clear and set."

2. This chapter includes three specific diagnostic questions one might ask regarding the Sabbath. How might these three questions be asked if the subject were:

    a. Health.

    b. State of the Dead.

    c. Gift of Prophecy.

3. Seven major decisions must be made to become a Seventh-day Adventist. Look at these seven in the light of a specific person you are now working with. Which ones did you fail to "clear and set" before moving to another subject?

9
The Understanding:
Perceptual Patterns

Successful soul winners are sensitive to the use of language. Would-be soul winners rely on glib religious phrases and clichés, without considering differing personalities. Remember, each listener has a unique perceptual set. Use it to win that person. Ignore it and you may lose the perspective convert.

Three Perceptual Sets
Students of human behavior place men and women in one of three classes: visual, audio, and kinesthetic.

Visuals solve problems by seeing the solution in the form of pictures in the mind. Since their analytical thought processes are visual, such people respond well to slides or charts and diagrams. They are the kind of people who, when thinking about a vacation, see themselves on the beach relaxing. They picture the glint of sunlight on sand and water. Their minds think in pictures like a constantly running video tape.

Audios, however, structure their thought patterns around the mode of sound. The husband hears his wife talking to him; the boss shouting at him; the children's voices as they play. He does not picture himself sitting in the shade or lounging on the beach when he thinks of vacation, but he hears the sweet music coming over the radio, the sound of surf pounding on rocks. His predominant sense is hearing.

Thought patterns of *kinesthetic* center largely around the mode of *touch.* They relate well to back patting, embracing, or solid handshakes. Thinking of their vacation, they feel the warm sun soaking into their bodies, the exhilaration of the cold plunge into the ocean.

Naturally, most people do not fall exclusively into one of these categories. Yet, each of us does have a tendency to operate primarily within the realm of one of these three sense impressions. The implications for soul winning are obvious. When dealing with an individual who sees things in his mind, my most effective approach will not be to plug in a tape recorder, but to set up a slide projector.

Jesus Reached All Three Sets

Perfectly tuned in to the personalities of those around Him, Jesus demonstrated His ability to reach different people by different means.

When conversing with those who were *visually* oriented, He painted pictures in rich hues to illustrate His message. He talked of the shepherd going out to find his sheep; the man hunting for the treasure hidden in a field; the prodigal's father running to his son with tear-stained cheeks. As they listened, people saw the message of the gospel in panoramic scenes before them and felt the answering chord of response.

When speaking to Nicodemus, Jesus used an *audio* appeal. Knowing his background as a Pharisee, his custom of listening to the reading of the law, Jesus said, "The wind blows where it wills, and you hear the sound of it, but you do not know whence it comes" (John 3:8 RSV). Jesus knew that as surely as Nicodemus could hear the sound of leaves rustling before a storm, and hear it whistling around the corners of his house, he could hear the calling of the Holy Spirit to his heart.

The woman at the well, having gone through six husbands, still did not feel the *touch* of love. Jesus knew just how to reach the core of her being. Appealing to her on the basis of feeling, He said simply, "Give me to drink." She knew the feeling of thirst, this woman who had trodden dusty roads in a desert land and lowered earthen pots into the waiting cool of darkness. Jesus used the kinesthetic sense impression to bring to her the strength and vitality of the gospel. "You have a thirst. If you drink the water I'll give you, you'll never thirst again."

Similarly, we can tailor our presentation of the gospel when sharing God's Word with people in the twentieth century. In public we should use all three approaches, for all three types of people are sure to be in the audience. It's wise to begin by appealing to all three sense impressions, then eventually focus on the one that appears to be the predominant mode of perception.

Appealing to the Visual

When speaking with visually-oriented persons, I emphasize my message in pictorial scenes:

"Picture Jesus dying on the cross for you, with nails through

His hands and blood trickling down His cheeks. As you look into His eyes, is there anything more important than surrendering your whole life to Him?"

"Imagine the smile on Jesus' face as you are baptized on Sabbath. See the angels as they gather around the Father's throne to witness your baptism."

"Visualize what it will be like to walk through those heavenly gates and down the streets of gold. Think of the splendor of heaven, the bright flowers, crystal streams, and gates of pearl."

Appealing to the Audio

For the audio, I tie the message into the sense of hearing: "Don't you hear Christ calling you today?"

"Think of that glorious angel chorus and that loud, clear trumpet fanfare! What a joy those sounds will bring to your heart."

"Listen to the voice of Jesus as He says, 'Well done, my good and faithful servant.'"

Appealing to the Kinesthetic

When speaking with a kinesthetic person my conversation might go something like this:

"As you surrender your life to Jesus you will receive that healing peace, that inner contentment that all humanity longs for. The feeling of peace that you desired for so long will be yours."

"The decision that you are about to make will lead you on a path with Jesus Christ where you'll feel His hand in yours, sense His leading, step by step."

"As the water covers you in baptism you will experience a wonderful sense of sins covered, of cleanness, and a removal of all guilt. Oh, you may not have a feeling of electrical energy going up your spine, but you can perceive the arms of Christ around you. You can sense the warmth of His embrace."

Jesus has created each individual to be unique. Each has come out of a different environment. This variety of backgrounds necessitates a variety of approaches. One reason we have so few outstanding soul winners is because most appeal to others in terms of their own perception. People wrapped up in themselves makes a small package and a poor soul winner! You must step out of yourself. You must enter into the needs and longings of others and identify with their perceptual patterns. Allow God to tune you in to others. Watch results multiply.

Continuing Education Assignment

1. What is your own perceptual set: visual, audio, or kinesthetic? Remember, you are a combination of all three—but which is most dominant? least dominant?

2. How do you find out what a listener's perceptual set might be?

3. Choose one of the following and using appropriate texts, phrase an appeal for:
   a. a visually-oriented college student to accept Christ.
   b. a kinesthetic, single mother to accept the Sabbath.
   c. an audio, retired subway conductor to be baptized.

10

The Indispensable:
Visitation Strategies

As the pastor related thestory, I suddenly felt sick. One of our outstanding evangelistic interests, who was preparing for the coming Sabbath's baptism, abruptly dropped out of our evangelistic meetings. She announced that she was severing her relationship with Adventists. She made the straightforward demand, "Pastor, please don't visit me. My mind is made up. My decision is final."

What could we do? Should we violate her request? Should we attempt to visit her when she had told us not to?

As the pastor and I discussed it, the thought struck me that she had told the pastor not to visit, but she had not told me that. Was the impression from the Holy Spirit? Was it just wishful thinking?

The conviction began to grow that I should visit her. After praying about it that evening, I went to sleep assured that it was God's will for me to see her the next day.

With a prayer in my heart, I made my way through her gate and onto her front porch. Just as I rang the doorbell, two large dogs—a German Shepherd and a Collie—rounded the corner behind me. Seeing me on the porch, they began to bark ferociously. Fear gripped me. Immediately I thought, "There's no hope. They are going to bite me." In desperation I sent another prayer heavenward—"O Lord, help me!"

Again I rang the bell. The dogs drew closer. Peeping out the window, Jane saw me. She hesitated but hearing the dogs, she opened the door a crack. That crack was all I needed. In my fear, I pushed the door as hard as I could and jumped inside the house. As I shut the door behind me, I breathed in relief, "Just like Daniel in the lion's den, the Lord delivered me."

Jane started laughing, but I was seized by embarrassment. I suddenly realized what I had done—I had barged into her house when she wanted me to stay out. Red-faced, I apologized, "Will

you please forgive me? I usually don't break into people's homes."
She laughed and said, "Wow! You're here. Although I wouldn't have let you in, you might as well stay. Sit down, please."

We talked. Or I should say she talked and I listened. At the appropriate times I asked questions. I began to sense that her response was not because she did not believe the doctrines we had presented but because of great pressure from her family.

About halfway through our conversation, her daughters joined us. Later, her husband came home from work. In her eagerness, she had been pressuring them. Because she was asking them to make a commitment that they were unprepared to make, they had become upset.

As both parties understood that God has given to each individual the freedom to choose, harmony replaced the tension in that home. The door that had previously been shut to a decision was re-opened. The hindrances gone, Jane followed through with her commitment. She came back to our meetings, was eventually baptized, and became a deaconess in one of our churches.

The Importance of Personal Visitation

It was a personal visit that made the difference. I am convinced that the effectiveness of evangelism depends on the establishment and cultivation of meaningful relationships through personal visitation. It is the lack of personal work that renders ineffective many of our efforts. Ellen White concurs with this observation:

> Your success will not depend so much upon your knowledge and accomplishments, as upon your ability to find your way to the heart. By being social and coming close to the people, you may turn the current of their thoughts more readily than by the most able discourse.
> —*Evangelism*, p. 437

The same author adds this important concept:

> The harder part comes after he [the minister] leaves the desk, in watering the seed sown. The interest awakened should be followed up but personal labor—visiting, holding Bible readings, teaching how to search the Scriptures, praying with families and interested ones, seeking to deepen the impression made upon hearts and consciences.
> —*Testimonies*, Vol. 5, p. 255

It is the neglect of this personal work—which is so costly in time, energy, and commitment—that limits the success of many seminars and evangelistic meetings. Mass evangelism without personal effort is destined to fail.

In his book, *Making Friends For Christ,* Wayne McDill reports on a survey of 4,000 viewers of religious TV programming. The question raised was, "How many of these viewers converted through TV ministries became a part of the local church?" The answer less than 1 percent.

Why is it that so few, who have made commitments to Christ through TV ministries, become a part of the local church? The basic reason is that they have not had the benefit of personal work. When relationships are not built with the new convert, the transition from personal commitment to active faith is difficult. As men and women grow in Christ, questions loom in their minds. The new converts may find attempting to live the Christian life in today's world discouraging. Unanswered questions, fears, and doubts may begin to choke out their seedling experience. Conversions that were genuine die on the vine.

A study of Billy Graham's Seattle evangelistic crusade supports this premise. Thirty percent of the 18,136 responses in that crusade were considered to be conversions. Only 15 percent of those converted were in the church one year later. Eighty-five percent either did not come to church or came for a short while and dropped out. The amazing thing is this: eight out of 10 of those who were in church a year later had developed a close relationship with someone who was already in the church.

Public proclamation is effective when it is wedded to personal visitation. As Jesus said regarding another subject, "What therefore God hath joined together, let not man put asunder." (Matthew 19:6)

Why isn't there more personal visitation? Why is it that some pastors and laymen spend most of their time preparing for and then conducting the public meeting rather than being involved in personal work?

Personal visitation is costly. It takes time and energy. It can be emotionally draining. McDill makes this telling point:

> This kind of evangelism [personal visitation] is costly, not in money or equipment, but in personal commitment. Relational evangelism, the missing ingredient, is a matter of trust and credibility, a matter of personal responsibility, a willingness to pay the high price of personal involvement, of emotional risk. It is the price of love.
> —*Making Friends for Christ,* p. 15

Using this powerful principle can increase the results your soul-winning ministry yields. Ignoring it can result in a well-attended seminar producing meager results.

The Purpose of Personal Visitation

Evangelistic visitation has *five purposes*. I call these purposes the five E's of effective visitation.

First, visitation will enable you to *establish relationships* that cannot be established in the public meeting. To this end, it is paramount that in your visitation you listen sensitively to the other person. Dietrich Bonhoffer put it well when he said, "The first service we owe to man is to listen to him."

If your visitation strategy is to dump a truckload of truth on people, hoping that they will respond, you will be bitterly disappointed. If you approach the individual with whom you are working as a prospect to be convinced or from the standpoint of a salesman with a product to sell, they may raise a wall of resistance. Listening is the key that unlocks another person to your influence. It is guaranteed to work if it is used prayerfully and sincerely. If you genuinely listen to other people and are interested in them, they will be open and receptive to your presentation of the gospel.

Most people are tuned to one channel—*self*. They become bored if you talk about yourself. They are awaiting an opportunity to discuss the things that are important to them. They are concerned about their jobs, health, future, financial security, husband, wife, hobbies, and generally the things that pertain to their lives. By providing them an opportunity to discuss what concerns them, you can begin to establish a relationship with them.

Many years ago I pastored a little country church in New England. The husband of one of the members there was not a Seventh-day Adventist. On one of my first Sabbaths in the church, she warned me never to visit her home. She was convinced that if I did, her husband would literally throw me out.

After carefully considering all the alternatives I decided to risk a visit. Without announcing my intentions, I simply appeared at their door one day. He was absolutely startled. He wondered why I had come. He was angered, yet out of courtesy he let me in. Upon entering their home, I noticed his gun collection displayed on one wall. Although I had never been interested in guns, I began to ask him questions about them—you do not have to know a lot about something to ask questions. I asked about the kinds of guns he had, their varying uses, the history of each one, and how he first became interested in collecting guns.

Before the afternoon was over he had taken me out to try some target shooting, and a friendship had begun. Soon this man who had been so bitterly opposed to his wife's attending the Adventist church began coming with her. He had needed someone to listen, to show an interest in him.

How to Listen

How do you listen? The obvious answer is with you ears. The word **EAR** provides an acronym that can be helpful in remembering what makes effective listening.

The E is for the *expression* on your face. If your eyes are wandering around the room, if the expression on your face indicates boredom, the person talking will not believe you are listening no matter what you say.

The **A** stands for *attention.* Direct the conversation away from yourself. Consciously remind yourself, "I am interested in this person. What is said matters to me. I desire to be tuned into this individual's frequency and not my own."

The **R** in our acronym reminds us that effective listeners *respond* appropriately. Effective listeners ask questions. Effective listeners draw the other person out. Effective listeners perceptively analyzes not only what the person says, but what the person means. Effective listeners find out whether they have understood the other person accurately by repeating what was said in other words and asking if their understanding is correct.

McDill states:

In a world where so few listen with sincere interest in one another, what a rare and welcome find a genuine listener would be. For a Christian seeking entrance into another's life, here is the key. Sincere listening says eloquently I care about you. Its a matter of deliberately switching channels to guide the conversation into other people's interest. It means forfeiting the right to talk about yourself. It means cultivating listening skills—looking your friend in the eye, paying attention to what he says, asking pertinent questions, nodding, smiling, and commenting briefly.
—Making Friends for Christ, p. 59.

If you are going to be an effective evangelist today, you must listen to other people. Listening actually helps you in two ways: it helps you determine the attitude and priorities of the person with whom you are dealing—an understanding essential to effectively ministering the gospel to that person. And listening helps you to establish a bond of friendship. It deepens your relationship with the other person.

The second purpose of visitation is to enable you to *evaluate interests.* Farmers must constantly make decisions. How is the fruit progressing? When will it be ready? Which fruit is ripe now?

Effective evangelists know how to evaluate and determine when the "fruit" is ripe. They are wise enough to leave "on the vine" a little longer those individuals who are not ready for harvesting. And it is through personal visitation that you can ascertain who of those attending your meetings are genuinely interested. I once worked with a pastor who was an extremely hard worker. Each week he put in well in excess of 55 hours. But his results were nowhere commensurate with the effort he put forth. As I visited with him, I observed that he lacked the ability to discriminate between a curiosity-seeker, one who was just taking up his time, and a genuine interest.

Many years ago I realized that I could not meet the needs or answer the questions of everyone coming to my meetings. So I concluded that my major responsibility was to discover where God was already working, whose hearts the Holy Spirit had already opened, whose minds He had already prepared. If you spend most of your time and effort with those who are not very interested right now, you will miss many people who are.

How to Discover Good Interest

How can you discover who your good interests are? Let me share a few of the criteria I use. First, good interests are generally *regular in their attendance* at the meetings. I recognize, of course, that some of those who come irregularly may be good interests. But the best interests are regular attenders. It is these people to whom I give top priority.

Second, good interests are *not generally debaters*. They ask intelligent questions and are satisfied with adequate answers.

Third, good interests regularly *have a positive, not a negative attitude*, toward the meetings and Bible studies. If an individual I am working with tends to be negative and highly critical of the meetings and message, I do not give top priority to visiting him. Generally, good interests have an open mind, they have a desire for truth. They want to do what God wants them to do. They are open to change and willing to consider new ideas.

One of the outstanding tests of whether an individual is a good interest is, fourthly, how much *spiritual progress* they are making. Has this individual relinquished any previous ideas upon learning new truths from the Bible, made any changes in lifestyle, given up any habits?

People's current lifestyles do not determine whether or not they are good interests. Some professed Christians are genuinely satisfied with their present experience and do not desire more truth. Because they may be living a good, moral life you may be tempted to think that they are good interests, but they may not be at all. I would much rather study with a persons whose lifestyles leave much to be desired if the Holy Spirit has been working on their hearts and they are open to the gospel.

I once studied the Bible with a man who smoked incessantly while I was there. Often, he and his wife each had a bottle of beer as well. They kept the TV turned up loud to entertain their three crying children. It was a horrendous atmosphere in which to conduct Bible studies. Yet these people had a genuine spiritual interest. As the weeks and months passed, one bad habit after another dropped off. Slowly, but steadily, they were moving toward Christ.

To evaluate the interests who are coming to my meetings, I ask a series of questions that are non-threatening, that leave people open, friendly, and receptive. The questions may go something like this: "Are you enjoying the seminar?" "Have you ever attended a seminar like this before?" "What has impressed you most about this seminar?" "Have you learned anything new in the seminar?" "Has the seminar caused you to make any changes in your life?"

Posing these questions early in my visitation program enables me to find out what is going on in the heart and mind of the interest. During these first few visits I am concerned about establishing relationships and evaluating interests. As I determine who the most outstanding interests are, I give them top priority in time and attention.

The third E of effective visitation means that I intend to *educate prospects* by answering their questions. Whereas in the first few visits I ask questions to draw out the prospects, as the meetings progress, I am particularly interested in answering questions that arise in my prospects' minds. Ellen White gives us one of the reasons why many evangelistic workers are not successful:

> *Many a laborer fails in his work because he does not come close to those who most need his help. With the Bible in hand, he should seek in a courteous manner to learn the objections which exist in the minds of those who are beginning to inquire, "What is truth?" Carefully and tenderly should he educate them as pupils in a school.*
> —Gospel Workers, p. 190.

> *Jesus reached souls because He was acquainted with their problems. His teachings were adapted to their situation. He understood the objection in their minds*   —Gospel Workers, p. 290

She further states:

> *The minister must know the nature of the difficulties in the minds of the people that he may know how to give every man his portion in due season.*
>
> —Manuscript 4, 1893.

Diagnostic Questions

The art of asking diagnostic questions is absolutely essential to discover the prospect's questions and to deal effectively with objections.

The fourth E is closely related to the third. In our visitation, we must not only educate the prospect by answering his questions, we must *entertain and disarm* the objections that he might raise.

When I visit an individual who has just heard a Bible presentation on Christ's second coming, I might raise the following questions: "Have you ever heard a presentation on Christ's second coming like the one at the seminar last evening?" "Was the message clear to you or do you have some questions about it?" "What do you think about what you heard?" "Does it seem to make sense to you?"

These are not threatening questions. They do not ask what the individual is going to do about what he has learned, nor do they ask him to make a commitment or to change his life-style. Before we ask people to make that kind of a tangible response, we must discover what they know about the subject and what convictions they hold on to.

Appropriate questions to ask after the meeting presenting Jesus as the Saviour of the world might include: "Do you see Jesus as a prophet, a historical figure, a religious teacher, or do you see Jesus as the divine Son of the living God, one who offers you eternal life?" "Were you brought up in a Christian home?" "Have you always been a Christian?" "Is it clear to you that Christ is the Messiah of the world?"

After the presentation on the Sabbath you might ask: "Is this the first time you have ever heard a message on the Sabbath?" "Is the Sabbath new to you?"

Diagnostic questions are not designed to stimulate action. They are especially designed to discover what the person knows, his attitude, and convictions. If diagnostic questions are used properly, they can be a great help to the evangelist.

Diagnostic questions must be used with care, however. If they are framed in such a way as to contain the answer in the question, or if the questions attempt to insinuate action, they can prematurely prejudice the individual. For example, the question "Isn't the Sabbath truth wonderful?" might be quite threatening. In asking it, I have asserted that the Sabbath is true. At this point I do not know whether the individual believes it or not. Also, I have assumed that the Sabbath truth is wonderful. If the person is working on the Sabbath or is a Sunday-keeping Christian, the Sabbath may not be perceived to be wonderful at all. I am not suggesting that this in an illegitimate question; what I am suggesting is that it is wrongly used at this point.

The final E of our visitation program is intended to *encourage decisions*. We can only proceed to this stage after we have carefully carried out the previous four stages: we have *established relationship, evaluated interests, educated* our prospects by answering their questions, and *entertained their objections*.

How to Encourage Decisions
In this process of effectively encouraging decisions I keep the three P's in mind. First, what is the individual's *previous knowledge?* Second, what is the person's *present understanding?* And third, is the person *ready to make a positive commitment?*

Let's suppose that it is week number two of our seminar. I am visiting with a person just after I have presented the gospel in the public meeting. In my visit, I review the essential elements of salvation. My desire is first, to discover the person's *previous knowledge*. What does he know of the way to salvation? I would ask something like: "Have you always been a Christian?" "Were you brought up in a Christian home?"

Second, I want to evaluate the person's *present understanding*. Does this individual visualize himself/herself as a Christian or as being outside of Christ? Appropriate questions would include: "Is it clear to you that Christ is more than a good man, more than a prophet, more than a moral-ethical teacher?" "Do you understand that Christ is the divine Son of God?" "Is it clear to you that Christ has offered eternal life to you—personally?"

And, third, if this person has not made a *significant commitment* to Christ, I would want to lead him/her to such a commitment. I might ask, Is there any good reason why you would not like to surrender your life to Jesus Christ now? Or, would you like to tell Jesus that you are giving Him your life and that today you want to receive the gift of eternal life? Is there anything standing between you and this decision?

Notice the progression in our visit. We have talked about the *past* and *previous knowledge, present understanding,* and *commitment for the future.*

This same pattern can be followed regarding the Sabbath. Let us assume that it is week number four or five in my Revelation Seminar. I have presented the Sabbath. Within 48 hours of that presentation, I attempt to visit each person that has heard it. I clarify the Sabbath doctrine in the context of a warm, loving relationship.

I ask such questions as: "Have you ever heard a message on the Sabbath before?" "Was the Sabbath totally new for you?" "Is it clear to you from the Bible that the Sabbath—the seventh day of the week, Saturday—is God's day of rest and worship?" "Do you have any questions regarding the Sabbath?"

After we openly discuss the Sabbath and any questions they have about the doctrine, I then ask: "What would it mean for you personally if you decide to keep the Sabbath? Let us suppose you were going to keep it. Would you have a problem keeping the Sabbath because of your work? Would it bring hardship to your family? What would it mean personally?"

As we discuss this change, I will ask this question: "If Jesus were here and personally declared, 'If you love me, keep my commandments,' how would you respond?" Recently in England, I went through this process with an Anglican. The Sabbath was new to him, yet he was convicted that it was biblical truth. Recognizing that accepting it would mean changing churches, he was extremely resistant. He had little desire to keep it.

Then I asked, "If Jesus were here and said, 'If you love me, keep my commandments,' and if Jesus himself invited you to keep the Sabbath, what would you say to Jesus?"

Putting his head in his hands, he thought for awhile. Then, looking up, he said, "Mark, if Jesus invited me to keep it, I suppose I would keep it."

Immediately I responded, "Let's pray together and ask Jesus to make His will plain to you."

We knelt, prayed, and within a week this brother was keeping the Sabbath. He has since been baptized. Confronted with the question, "What would you do if Jesus were here and He asked you to keep the Sabbath?" he was led to decision and commitment.

At this stage of our visitation, it is sometimes necessary to ask direct questions. Lovingly phrased question may stimulate the person to action. The desire to obey Christ will lead many committed Christians to follow truth. As they understand that Jesus and His truth are inseparable, they will be willing to make life-changing decisions.

There are scores of people who will not make a personal commitment to Christ and His truth unless you visit them in their homes. The most effective evangelists are those who realize the immense value of personal visitation. It is amazing what the Holy Spirit can do in hearts and lives when we visit people in their homes.

Effective evangelists *look at people through the eyes of Christ*. They see the faith potential in each individual. They recognize that as people come to the public meetings, have their questions answered through personal visitation, and are led to a deep commitment to Jesus and His truth, they will experience miraculous changes.

Successful evangelists believe that God is at work on earth building His kingdom in the hearts of men and women. They believe that many an unlikely prospect will be won through their efforts. Jesus saw potential in a cheating tax collector, Zacchaeus. He saw potential in a hardened Roman soldier, a demon-possessed man and an adulteress. Jesus spent time with a loud-mouthed fishermen by the name of Peter, a leader of the religious opposition by the name of Nicodemus, and a young thief who hung on the cross next to Him.

Jesus addressed men and women about the subject of salvation individually. He confronted men and women with the claims of the Eternal. Jesus saw men and women not as they were but as they might become when refined and ennobled by His grace. In public proclamation and personal visitation, the Holy Spirit's power flowed through Jesus and touched other lives. Jesus saw the potential in each individual He met.

One January, my wife and I held a nutrition series in one of the cities on the east coast of the United States. A woman who began attending came with an old woolen hat pulled down over her ears and a faded tattered overcoat wrapped around her. We noticed that after each nutrition class, she searched the garbage cans for discarded morsels of food. She often took three or four platefuls home with her.

She seemed an extremely unlikely candidate for the spiritual truths we had to offer. Yet a very compassionate young man on our evangelistic team spent time getting acquainted with her. He took the initiative to visit this woman and her husband in their home. Soon they became friends. As a result, they accepted his invitation to attend our evangelistic meetings. When the meeting concluded, however, they were still unprepared for baptism. This couples' background was such that they needed extended personal attention.

About a year later I visited that area and spoke at a youth meeting in the same church. During the song service, the fine quality of music impressed me. I particularly noticed the pianist—a nicely dressed, middle-aged woman. Then I looked again. I could hardly believe it! The pianist was the woman who had been eating food out of the garbage can the year before! What outstanding growth in only a year. She had become a part of the church. Now she proudly participated in the youth meeting through her gift of music.

Our public meetings alone were not enough. But one of our staff recognized the importance of visiting at home, of supplementing the public presentation with personal visitation. He saw this woman's potential.

Do you have that 20/20 vision? Do you see that you must combine personal work with public proclamation? This is the missing ingredient in our evangelism. Discovered, it can make all the difference between success and failure.

Continuing Education Assignment

1. To be effective in visitation one must be a good listener. Using the acrostic E-A-R summarize what it means to be a good listener.

2. Identify the attitudes and behavior patterns you find in a good interest.

3. Write a series of diagnostic questions to lead your interests to decisions on the following subjects:

    a. Acceptance of Jesus as Saviour.

    b. The Sabbath.

    c. The State of the Dead.

11

The Appeals:
Increasing Results

A number of years ago, Robert L. Boothby held a major evangelistic campaign in Washington D.C. A number of young Adventist pastors worked with the campaign, learning the art of evangelism. One evening after the meeting, one of the young pastors met Elder Boothby in the hallway. He inquired, "Elder Boothby, what is the secret of success in getting decisions for Christ? How can I make my appeals more effective? Why do you have so many decisions for Christ while I have only a few?"

Boothby thought for a moment, then in his gentle but very earnest manner inquired, "Young man you don't expect to get a decision every time you preach do you?"

The young pastor responded, "Not every time, Elder Boothby. But I would like to get more decisions than I am and that is why I have come to you tonight."

As quick as a flash Boothby replied, "Until you preach as if you expect someone to make a decision that very night, you will get very few decisions."

What wisdom! God has placed within every audience men and women who are prepared to make a decision. The purpose of preaching is not simply to inform the intellect. It is not merely to enlighten the mind. Evangelistic preaching means to lead men and women to decisions for Christ.

The making of appeals is essential to fulfilling the purpose of evangelistic preaching. Making appeals is biblical. It is part of God's plan for saving humanity. God Himself appealed to rebellious Adam in the Garden of Eden by calling out in tones of tenderest love, "Where art thou, Adam?" (Gen. 3:9). As Israel drifted into open rebellion against God, Moses called them to decision. He asked directly, "Who is on the Lord's side?" (Ex. 32:26). And Joshua again gave Israel the opportunity to decide with the words, "Choose you this day whom ye will serve." (Josh. 24:15).

Jesus called men and women publicly. And, as the Spirit of God ministered through Jesus, touching the hearts and minds of people, they affirmed their faith in public. Jesus called Matthew while he was sitting at the receipt of custom with his friends. He called Peter from mending fishing nets by the Sea of Galilee. He called Zacchaeus while he was sitting on the limb of a tree, and Zacchaeus responded by openly affirming his faith in Christ.

With the crowds thronging Him, Jesus called a woman in the crowd to commitment by asking, "Who touched Me?" Have you ever wondered why Jesus asked that question, why He wanted her to respond publicly? Wasn't He putting pressure on her? Might not His question embarrass her? Jesus knew that *expression deepens impression*. He recognized that when men and women publicly affirm their faith in Christ, their faith is strengthened.

Of Paul, Acts says, "He reasoned in the synagogue every sabbath and persuaded the Jews and the Greeks" (Acts 18:4; see also Acts 19:8). As the apostles reasoned with men and women regarding the truths of God's Word, they called them to decision. Their purpose was not merely to proclaim but to persuade. It was not merely to convince, but to convert. The purpose of preaching is to lead to decision.

Dr. Charles W. Koller remarks:

> *The supreme test of all preaching is what happens to the man in the pew. To John the Baptist there was accorded the highest tribute to a minister of the gospel: when they heard John they followed Jesus.*
> —Expository Preaching Without Notes, p. 19

Evangelistic Preaching and Seminar Teaching Contrasted

I have been involved in seminar evangelism for a number of years. During that time, my wife and I have conducted many kinds of seminars: Five Day Plans to Stop Smoking, stress seminars, parenting seminars, nutrition series, and Daniel and Revelation seminars. Although because of their biblical and Christ-centered nature the religious seminars carry with them more appealing power than do the health seminars, I have observed that in a seminar it is difficult to make appeals that elicit a public response. Certainly it is possible to use decision questions and call for the participants to raise their hands in response. And if the seminar is quite large, one might even try a standing call. But it appears to me that the atmosphere in a seminar is quite different than that in a public evangelistic meeting.

During the appeal in a public evangelistic meeting, all of the decisional elements in the individual are brought into focus. Evangelistic preaching and evangelistic music create a setting in which the Holy Spirit can work upon the heart and lead to a decision. Seminars generally do not offer that kind of a setting.

Human beings are physical, mental, emotional, and spiritual beings. Any attempt to reach men and women that focuses particularly on the intellectual—which seminars naturally tend to do—is going to miss large numbers of people.

Some will argue that public evangelism is too emotional. They believe that decisions must be made by the intellect and that emotion has nothing to do with the decision. I certainly agree that some calls depend too much on the emotions. This is true of the evangelist who labors 20 or 30 minutes with emotional stories, taking advantage of his audience and manipulating their wills. When I talk about appealing to the whole person, I do not have this kind of tear-jerking, emotional appeal in mind.

Instead, I am thinking of the kind of call that was often made in the early Adventist church. Speaking of the Advent movement of 1843 and 1844, Ellen White describes the kind of call that lead sinners to true conversion:

Frequently a call would be made for those who believed the truths that were proved by the Word, to rise to their feet, and large numbers would respond. —Evangelism, p. 284

Notice the elements in this sentence. The appeal was made to the intellect—those who "believed the truths that were proved by the Word" were invited to respond. Emotion plays a part in the decision-making process, but it does not lead to the decision. When the individual is intelligently informed and is convicted of the truth, emotions prompt the will to make a decision.

Billy Graham speaks of the role of emotion in altar calls this way:

Some people accuse us of too much emotionalism. I say we have too little. That's why we are losing church people to other interests. We need not only to capture their minds but to touch their hearts. We've got to make people feel their faith.
—Billy Graham Speaks, p. 110

Spurgeon advised young preachers,

A sinner has a heart as well as a head. A sinner has emotions as well as thoughts, and we must appeal to both. A sinner will never be converted until his emotions are stirred, unless he feels sorrow for sin.
—Spurgeon the Soul Winner p. 126

Evangelistic Appeals

An evangelistic appeal has power to draw men and women to Christ. When an evangelist is burdened for souls and is filled with the Spirit of God, he stands before an audience and appeals to men and women to surrender their lives to Christ, the Holy Spirit witnesses to individual minds.

In earnestness, the evangelist may say, "God has spoken to you tonight. You have heard His voice. He is calling you tonight. Tonight He is saying, 'Come.'

"Don't put off this decision. Jesus is appealing to you. He says, 'I love you and want to forgive you.'

"The Holy Spirit has stirred your heart tonight. God may never speak as forcefully as He has done this evening. Picture the arms of Jesus. They are stretched out wide for you. He is beckoning for you to come tonight.

"Listen to His voice calling you now, 'My child, I love you. Come tonight. Come with your sins. Come with your weaknesses. Come with your fears. Come with your doubts.'

"Tonight, whoever you are—salesman, housewife, factory worker, business executive, student—come to Jesus. Tonight, wherever you are, in the front or in the back or on the side of this auditorium, come to Jesus. He will accept you tonight. He will forgive you tonight. He speaks to your heart tonight.

"Come now, as we sing that marvelous hymn 'Come every soul of sin oppressed, There's mercy with the Lord.' Notice particularly the chorus, 'Only trust Him, Only trust Him, Only trust Him now.' If you want to say to Jesus, 'I'm trusting You and I'm trusting You now,' come —and come now."

There is power in that kind of appeal. The Holy Spirit uses it to prompt people to come forward. Personally, I believe in and use decision cards, but decision cards do not appeal to some kinds of people; they pass them by each evening.

A number of years ago I was holding an evangelistic series in Pittsfield, Massachusetts. During the series I repeatedly used decision cards. As the decision cards were distributed, I invited men and women to check the appropriate box if the message of the evening was clear. I encouraged them to respond to the truths that they were hearing.

One particular individual attending our meetings, whose wife was an Adventist, had for many years had a problem with alcohol. Faithfully his wife sought God for his soul during those years. Each evening he came to the meeting out of respect for her, but showed little interest. I noted particularly that he passed the decision cards to the person next to him. He was hesitant to make any commitment.

Throughout the meetings he gave no indication of a positive response. Finally, at the close of one of the meetings, I gave a Spirit-filled call. As he heard the call, he got up and came forward. God's Spirit had impressed him that night. He sensed that for him that was decision night. I doubt whether that man ever would have made his decision if we had only used cards. It took the dynamic of a Spirit-filled altar call, with the Spirit working upon his emotions as well as his intellect, to draw from him a response.

On another occasion, a lady told me, "Pastor, as I thought about making a decision, I resisted. During your call I resisted. But during that call, I sensed the Holy Spirit speaking to my heart. I could resist no longer, so I stood."

The Psychology of Appeals

R.J. Fish makes this observation about the psychological soundness of the appeal:

> *By man's make up, he needs the opportunity to respond to the gospel. Someone has well said that impression without expression can lead to depression. To preach for response and to fail to provide an opportunity for a commitment can frustrate those who hear the gospel and deepen them in their habit of procrastination.*
> —*Giving a Good Invitation*, p. 10

Hearing the message of God creates within the individual a desire to respond. If the individual does not respond, cannot respond because no avenue for response has been provided, it becomes much more difficult for him to respond in the future.

Social psychologists declare that there is a high correlation between intention to act and actual behavior. The stronger the intention to act, the more likely it is that action will follow. But here is a vital key. Time is a major factor affecting the correlation of action with decision. The greater the interval between the decision and the action desired, the less likely it is that the person will take that action.

So appealing for people to accept Christ and then giving them a week to decide is an immense mistake. During that interval, the effectiveness of the appeal will diminish. Inviting people who believe the Sabbath to attend church the very next Sabbath strengthens their resolve and leads them to decision.

Individuals should be led to make a decision as soon as 1)

they have sufficient knowledge to make the decision, 2) all their major objections have been met, and 3) they believe that it is what God wants them to do and they are convicted that God is leading them to make the given decision. The longer the time lapses between their being convicted and their taking action, the less likely they are to take that action.

I would certainly acknowledge that there are a variety of ways in which the individuals can respond to appeals. They may respond, for instance, by filling out a response sheet or card, by raising a hand, by standing, or by coming forward. Nevertheless, it appears to me that God has designed the human mind in such a way that a visible, specific response is strengthening and highly beneficial for most people.

Billy Graham has quite a collection of letters from psychologists who approve of his alter call. Apparently, these psychologists recognize that human beings innately need to express inner convictions in outer action.

Robert Sumner concludes that all logic is against telling someone to do something without pressing him to act immediately. (Letter to Al Street June 30, 1981) A. E. Grundstaff adds,

Nothing is more cruel and damaging to distract people religiously than to make them ready for a decision and fail to give an invitation to register the decision. —The Effective Invitation, p. 146

Another psychological factor to be considered when appealing to individuals to make a public decision is this: when an individual acts based on a given attitude, the attitude is strengthened. This is, in fact, one of the basic reasons why God has given us the ordinances of the church. As we rehearse the death of Christ in the communion service, the rehearsal impresses deeply upon our minds the meaning of the cross. As men and women make a public commitment to their Lord in baptism, resurrection takes place in their own hearts and lives. The ordinances of the church are more than symbolic. They are rich, dynamic experiences in the life of the believer. The more we act a certain way, the deeper our convictions will be.

Some time ago a study was done on moral values in grade school children. One aspect of the study had to do with cheating. At the beginning of the year, students were given a test to determine their attitudes toward cheaters. Among other things, the test asked what punishment the children thought cheaters should receive. All of the children were quite strict. Some prescribed heavy financial fines, some prescribed beatings and others expelling the cheaters from school.

About halfway through the year, the researchers gave a test especially designed to make it easy for children to cheat, which a number of them did. At the end of the year, the children were given the same test that they had taken at the beginning of the year. Then the scores of the two tests were correlated with the test given during the year to determine if there was any relationship between the act of cheating and the students' attitudes toward cheaters. The researchers found that at the end of the year, those children who cheated on the test were much more inclined toward leniency in regard to cheaters than they had been at the beginning of the year.

We had long known that attitudes affect actions. Now we see that actions affect attitudes as well. If you desire somebody to believe a certain way, provide opportunities for them to act in harmony with that belief. Such actions intensify and strengthen the belief. A person who, believing the Sabbath to be true, publicly acknowledges that belief and then begins keeping it, has a much stronger belief and deeper commitment than a person who believes but does nothing about it. Psychologically, the greater and more repeated the action, the deeper the attitude will be ingrained.

I once saw a cartoon depicting a man embracing his wife and repeatedly kissing her. The caption read, "I love you. I love you. I love you. I love you." Then in small print it said, "There I go, I've convinced myself." The act of kissing his wife deepened the love in his own heart. He loved her more after he kissed her than he had before.

Essential Elements in a Call

This leads us to an important practical question, How should a call be given? What are the essential elements of a call?

Spurgeon says that the most important element in a call is the *earnestness* of the individual giving the call. The audience must perceive that you believe that the call is significant, that you are in earnest about it, that God has given you an urgent message.

Before Billy Graham went to Scotland, he was told that it was impossible to make an invitation there. He was warned, "No one will respond." Throughout his sermon he struggled, wondering what to do. As he came to the conclusion, he, under the guidance of the Holy Spirit, made a direct appeal. At first no one moved. As he often does, Graham stood, arms folded, head bowed, praying. It was as if he were closed in with the Almighty.

Raising his head, looking out upon that great stadium, he noticed hundreds coming forward. The Scottish clergy sitting on the platform had tears in their eyes, sensing that his earnest, prayerful appeal had touched hearts.

Not only must the appeal be earnest and prayerful, it must be *clear*. Leighton Ford says:

> *When I ask people to come forward at the end of an evangelistic meeting, I try to make it clear what I'm asking them to do. At the beginning of the sermon I may say something like this, "Tonight at the end of my talk I'm going to ask you to do something about it, to express your decision. I'm going to ask you to get up and come and stand here in front. This is an outward expression of an inward decision. Just as you make a promise to someone, mean to keep it, and shake hands on it; just as a young couple come to love each other, want to give themselves to each other, and then openly express that covenant in a wedding, so I'm asking you to express your coming forward. Walking down here doesn't make you a Christian. You come down here a thousand times with your feet and it would make no difference at all if that's all it was. But as you come here with your feet, you are saying with your heart, God, I'm coming to you and leaving behind those things that are wrong and sinful. I'm trusting Christ as my Saviour and I'm coming to follow Him in this church from tonight on.*
>
> —"The Evangelistic Invitation" *Leadership,* Fall 1984.

People need to understand what the invitation means and what it does not mean. The call must be clear. Are you inviting people to accept Christ? Say so. Are you inviting them to prepare for the Second Coming of Jesus by surrendering some sinful habit? Tell them! Are you inviting people who once knew Christ to come back to Him? What about those who once used to be Adventists; are they being invited to return? If you are inviting people to keep the Sabbath, give up unclean foods, to be baptized, make that clear. Be sure, of course, that you do not include too many groups in a single call.

One of my typical calls goes something like this: "If you have never accepted Christ, I invite you to make that decision tonight. If at one time you had accepted Christ and you have drifted away or allowed some sin to control your life, come."

This particular call is effective early in an evangelistic series. Later in the series my call might be: "If you believe that you have been hearing the truth of God and are convicted that God wants you to follow it and you want to say, 'Yes, Jesus, I am going all the way with You and following Your truth,' I invite you now to get out of your seat and come forward."

For a call to be effective, the evangelist must have a sense of *urgency*. He must believe that there are people in the congregation that very night who will respond. In every discourse *fervent* appeals should be made to lead people to forsake their sins and turn to Christ. There is something about an evangelist with a sense of urgency that God can use to enable audiences to respond.

On October 8, 1871, Dwight Moody preached a sermon entitled "What Shall I Do With Jesus?" At the close of the sermon Moody said, "I want you to take the message home with you tonight and think about it. Next week when you return, I will invite you to make a decision for Christ." Then Ira Sankey began to sing, "Today the Saviour calls, for refuge fly; the storm of justice falls and death is nigh."

Sankey never finished the hymn. While he was singing, there came the rush and roar of fire engines on the street outside. Before morning Chicago lay in ashes. To his dying day Moody regretted that he told the congregation to come next week and decide what to do with Jesus. He said:

> *I have never dared to give an audience a week to think of their salvation since. If they were lost, they might rise up in the judgment against me. I have never seen that congregation since. I will never meet those people again until I meet them in another world. But I want to tell you of one lesson that I learned that night which I have never forgotten and that is, when I preach I press Christ upon the people right then and there and try to bring them to decision on the spot. I would rather have my right hand cut off than give an audience a week to decide what to do with Jesus.* —The Shepherd Evangelist, pp. 186, 187

Such urgency in appeals enables the Holy Spirit to work powerfully on hearts and minds.

A minister was preparing to preach to the inmates of a penal institution. The afternoon before he was to speak he visited the place. The warden showed him around, ending the tour at the chapel —a large auditorium seating about 1,500.

"It will be full tomorrow morning," the warden said.

Two seats on the front row were draped in black. When the preacher inquired about them, the warden replied, "The two men who will occupy those seats tomorrow are under the sentence of death. On Monday they will go to the electric chair."

"Under the sentence of death," repeated the minister quietly. Then he said, "Do I understand that this will be the last service they will ever attend?"

"Yes, sir," was the reply. "Your sermon will be the last one they will ever hear."

The preacher had seen all he wanted to. He must find a place to be alone and do some thinking. When he reached home he went to his study, took out the sermon he had prepared, reviewed it, and tore it up. "This is of no use," he said. "It does not meet the need."

Then falling on his knees, he prayed, "O God, give me a message for the two men who will be sitting in those draped chairs."

Brother, sister, there are draped chairs in every audience. Every time we preach we are looking into the eyes of men and women who are judgment-bound. We are speaking to men and women who are under the sentence of death.

If we are to reach men and women for Christ, our hearts must be filled with the Holy Spirit. Before their hearts break in sorrow for sin, our hearts must break in earnest confession of anything which hinders the outpouring of the Holy Spirit through us. Before we can effectively share the Bread of Life, we ourselves must receive it from the hand of Christ. Before we lead men and women to the cross, we must come to the cross and learn the terrible price of our sins. Only as our eyes are anointed with a vision of the soon coming of our Lord can we preach the reality of His coming to others. Our ability to lead others to decision for Christ is directly proportional to the depth of our own commitment.

Pastor, your role is not merely to tickle the intellectual curiosity; your role is not to expound on the teaching of truth. Your role is to lead men and women to know Christ, to instruct them in the principles of Christ, and to get them to decide to follow Christ. Never be satisfied with anything less.

Continuing Education Assignment

1. State your convictions regarding the use of emotion in appeals.

2. What key fact do most psychologists suggest regarding inner attitudes and some visible action?

3. Write out an appeal for baptism which includes the elements of motivation, conviction, and benefits. Be sure your appeal is clear, specific, urgent, and Christ-centered.

12

The Intercession:
Prayer Dynamics

Mike was troubled. About midway through an evangelistic series, three young girls who had been attending regularly approached him saying, "We have been looking into the Seventh-day Adventist Church, but just yesterday we talked with our pastor. We wanted to inform you tonight that we are not coming back. Here are the magazines and books you have given us."

As Mike drove home from the evangelistic meeting that evening, his thoughts were in a whirl. What could he do? Should he visit the girls? Should he call them? Their decision seemed so final. Deeply concerned, he drove to the church. It was 10:00 in the evening. He opened the door and sat down in the darkness of the sanctuary. Dropping to his knees, a great burden flowed from him for these three girls. As he prayed, earnestly pleading with God for their souls, a peace came over him. He did not know for certain how God was going to work, but he knew his prayer was answered. It was after midnight when he got back into the car and drove home.

Two days later, on Sabbath, as Mike was greeting visitors in the church foyer, he notice these three girls walking cautiously up the steps. In utter amazement he greeted them. "Girls! What are you doing here?"

Quickly they responded, "We just wanted to come and visit your church. Is it O.K.?"

For the next few weeks Mike watched as God kept impressing the girls to come back to the evangelistic meetings. Soon they were open to his Bible studies. Later, as they stood in the baptismal pool at the New Haven, Connecticut Adventist Church, he knew once again that the power of effective soul winning comes on our knees, pleading with God for the salvation of souls.

Recently on the "It Is Written" television program, I interviewed Larry Dorsey, the former chief of the medical staff of the

Dallas General Hospital. Dr. Dorsey has extensively studied the role of intercessory prayer in healing. After reviewing 130 medical studies in the last 25 years on the role of intercessory prayer in a patient recovering from a life-threatening disease, Dr. Dorsey has concluded that scientifically there is a dramatic difference when people are prayed for. If this is true in the physical realm of healing think of how much truer it is in the realm of spiritual healing—conversion.

Prayer + Faith = Souls

There are *two essential ingredients* in soul winning. I John 5:14-16 lists them both:

> *And this is the* confidence *that we have in him, that, if we ask anything according to his will, he heareth us: And if we know that he hear us, whatsoever we ask, we know that we have the petitions that we desired of him. If any man see his brother sin a sin which is not unto death, he shall ask, and he shall give him life for them that sin not unto death.*

Our passage reveals things about successful soul winning: the necessity of intercessory prayer, and the necessity of implicit faith.

Prayer and faith will do what no power on earth can accomplish.
—The Ministry of Healing, *p. 509*

It is a part of God's plan to grant us, in answer to the prayer of faith, that which He would not bestow did we not thus ask
—The Great Controversy, *p. 525*

Winning a soul is not like repairing an automobile or making a cake in which there is a certain formula, and anybody who follows it will be successful. No, each person is different, and although there are basic soul-winning principles which apply to every situation, we need the wisdom of God in applying them. Otherwise, minds will not be impressed. Lives will be left unchanged.

Prayer Empowered Christ

Scripture clearly reveals that Christ's power came from the secret place of prayer. He prayed in the wilderness of temptation when the adversary battled for His soul. He prayed the night before He selected His disciples. He prayed through the night before He delivered the nobleman's son from a demon. He prayed in Gethsemane before the cross.

Soul winners seem sometimes to think they are too busy to pray. Jesus did not.

And at even, when the sun did set, they brought unto him all that were diseased, and them that were possessed with devils. And all the city was gathered together at the door. And he healed many that were sick of divers diseases, and cast out many devils; and suffered not the devils to speak, because they knew him. And in the morning, rising up a great while before day, he went out, and departed into a solitary place, and there prayed. —Mark 1:32-35.

With the setting sun the whole city came, clamoring for His attention. What evangelist has ever been busier? But busy nights were not allowed to interfere with praying mornings. There was power at night because there was prayer in the morning.

Prayer Does Four Things

Why is it necessary to pray for souls? Doesn't God already want to win them? Isn't He doing everything He can without our praying? There is a great deal about the science of prayer that the human mind cannot comprehend. This should not discourage us. Simply because we do not understand all about electricity does not keep us from employing the benefits of light, heat, and the electrical power. In the late 1800s almost nothing was known about Vitamin B, yet an individual eating whole wheat bread received as much benefit from Vitamin B then as we do now. The point is simply this: It is not necessary to know everything about something to benefit from it.

Although we will never fully understand the science of prayer, there are four reasons we should pray for souls:

1. *Prayer enables God to speak to us about sins in our own lives which are a hindrance to successful soul winning.* The Israelites had just been defeated by the men from a tiny city called Ai. Joshua entered into earnest prayer over the situation, and God said, "Get thee up; wherefore liest thou thus upon they face? Israel hath sinned... Therefore the children of Israel could not stand before their enemies" (Joshua 7:10-12). God's power was limited because there was sin among His people. He used the prayer of Joshua as an opportunity to speak to him about sin.

Very often as you and I come to pray for others, Jesus impresses our own hearts with the need of a closer fellowship with Him. In the atmosphere of prayer, soul winning is the fulcrum by which Jesus pries sin out of our lives. We say, "Oh, Lord, I never saw myself that way before. If that is the way I really am, if my bitterness, my jealousy, my pride are standing between me and You, oh, Lord, take it away so You can effectively witness through me to win that soul." In prayer Jesus reveals to us attitudes that inhibit His working through us.

2. *Prayer deepens our desire concerning the thing for which we are praying.* One of the reasons Jesus does not immediately move into a life as we pray, is to enable us to come in such close harmony with Him that we will work harder with Him for the salvation of that particular soul. The more we pray for someone's salvation, the more we desire it. The more we desire it, the more we will look for creative opportunities to reach that person.

3 *Prayer puts us in touch with divine wisdom.* The only One who is really wise enough to win souls is God. "If any of you lack wisdom, let him ask of God" (James 1:5). Isaiah 50:4, speaking prophetically of Jesus, says, "The Lord God hath given me the tongue of the learned, that I should know how to speak a word in season to him that is weary." Only Jesus gives us the tongue of the learned. He reveals the right words to say to men and women. Without His wisdom we may have keys, but we do not know which key fits where. It is the wisdom of Jesus that chooses the right key to fit each particular heart and opens it to receive the treasures of the gospel.

4. *Prayer enables God to work more powerfully than He could if we did not pray.* Daniel 10 tells the story of how Daniel's prayers ascended to heaven for three weeks with no apparent answer. Yet at the end of those three weeks Gabriel explained to Daniel that a great battle had been going on over the mind of Cyrus. The good angels attempted to drive the evil angels back so that Cyrus could make the right decision. The evil angels attempted to destroy the good angels, to enshroud Cyrus in darkness. As Daniel prayed, this battle raged. Finally, Jesus came down, beat the evil angels back, and gave Cyrus an opportunity to make a clear and intelligent decision. Israel was allowed to go free. Daniel's intercessory prayer proved effective.

Isn't God doing everything He can to save a person before we pray? Yes. But when we pray as did Daniel it enables God to do more than He could have done before. God has voluntarily chosen to limit Himself in the great controversy between good and evil. He has chosen not to violate human will. When one human mind prays for another it enables Him to work on minds more dramatically than He otherwise could.

Pray Specifically

This mater of praying for souls is an individual work. It is not simply that we pray for a hundred names quickly on a pray list so something magic will happen. There are some forms of life for which multiple births are usual. An opossum, for instance, can give birth to a litter of a dozen or more. Not so with human beings. Occasionally we see twins born, and still more seldom, triplets or quadruplets. But most humans are born one at a time. And that's the way it is with soul winning. If you want to win souls, begin with one.

Notice the counsel that Job gives us in praying for souls: "O that one might plead for a man with God, as a man pleadeth for his neighbor." This is our work, pleading before God for the specific needs of John or Joseph, Mary or Alice. "God forbid that I should sin against the Lord in ceasing to pray for you" (1 Samuel 12:23). Do you have a prayer list? Are there men and women that you are holding up before God in prayer? Soul winning is God's work, not man's. Prayer opens our hearts and minds to be used as channels for the Holy Spirit's working.

Pray in Groups

In addition to praying alone for souls, notice the instruction Jesus gives us:

> *If two of you shall agree on earth as touching any thing that they shall ask, it shall be done for them of my Father which is in heaven. For where two or three are gathered together in my name, there am I in the midst of them.* —Matthew 18: 19, 20

Ellen White adds:

> *Why do not two or three meet together and plead with God for the salvation of some special one, and then still another?*
> —*Testimonies of the Church*, vol. 7, p. 21

These little prayer bands provide the basis for successful evangelism. The work of conversion is not natural; it is supernatural. A salesman might be able to persuade a person to buy a new car. Advertising companies may entice an individual to purchase a new suit of clothing. A real estate broker might interest a person in an attractive new home. These sales people can get results by following certain techniques. They can sell their product. It might even be possible for a Christian minister to persuade a person to join the church. But only God can being genuine conversion to the soul. Successful evangelism must include a ministry of prayer.

Develop a prayer list of specific individuals. Seek God for those people each day, write down their names, petition heaven for their souls. If possible choose a prayer partner. Together bombard heaven with your prayers. God will answer. You will become a channel of His abundant blessings. The river of the Water of Life will be poured out through you to touch another life for the Kingdom of God.

The New Testament reveals that evangelistic explosion throughout the book of Acts was the result of the mighty outpouring of the Holy Spirit.

Since we are living in the days of earth's final harvest, it is essential for the success of any evangelistic campaign that each of us consecrate ourselves to God for service, are of one accord and filled with the Holy Spirit.

Without prayer spiritual renewal is impossible. As public evangelists unite with local congregations in an integrated, coordinated approach in winning souls for Christ, praying for the mighty outpouring of the Holy Spirit, God will give us unusual results. The Spirit will be poured out and souls will be won.

Continuing Education Assignment

1. What relationship does intercessory prayer have to the great controversy between good and evil?

2. What specific plans are now in effect at your church to encourage prayer groups?

3. What plans for prayer groups would you like to see added?

4. The reason I do not pray for souls more than I do is:

13

The Hurdles:
Overcoming Bad Habits

Mary and John sat before me with looks of deep anguish upon their faces. It was John who spoke first, "What does it mean to be born again? How do you understand the Bible? What is the new birth?"

Almost as fast as the questions were fired, the cigarettes were lit, rapidly filling the room with smoke. I would not have considered the questions so unusual had not Mary and John been through a complete evangelistic series, an entire set of Bible studies, and hours of discussion on the new birth. John insisted, "We have just about come to the place where we are willing to give up this whole thing called Christianity. We can not understand how to be converted, what it means to be born again. We have been reading, and the more we read the more confused we get." With that, he lit another cigarette.

As we talked, I became increasingly aware that the major problem was not a failure to intellectually understand the Bible, conversion, or the new birth. John and Mary had known the truth of God for more than a year, yet could not conquer the smoking habit. And so I asked, "Would you please share with me the major spiritual problems that you are facing in your life right now? What is the number one problem that you think might be keeping you from a full experience with God? Do you have any habits in your life that are blocking that relationship?"

Almost without hesitation, John picked up the pack of cigarettes beside him. "Our smoking. We want to quit. We have tried to quit."

Soberly, Mary nodded her assent, "We just can't quit."

The frustration was apparent. John and Mary struggled not for an intellectual knowledge of the new birth, but for the victory over an ingrained and persistent habit.

To Act on Christ's Words Is to Be Healed
As we talked, I shared these thoughts with them:

"John and Mary, your problem is a serious one. Yet, as you study the New Testament it becomes obvious that there were people who had problems more serious than even the one you are facing; problems, that they too, were incapable of dealing with on their own. In John 5 the Bible tells us the story of the man at the Pool of Bethesda. He had been a helpless cripple for 38 years. He was discouraged and without hope. Then Jesus came, 'Wilt thou be made whole?' Do you *really* want to be healed?

"I think He would ask you a similar question. Do you really want to quit smoking? Do you really choose to give it up?' The impotent man raised an excuse in Verse 7, 'Sir, I have no man, . . . to put me into the pool: but while I am coming, another steppeth down before me.' In other words, 'I want to. But I can't.'

"Jesus answered in Verse 8, 'Rise, take up thy bed, and walk.' Jesus did not say to the man, 'Your sickness is *healed*, rise, take up they bed, and walk.' Jesus said, 'Rise, take up they bed, and walk.' It was necessary for that man to exercise faith in the miracle-working power of Jesus *before* the miracle could happen. Not faith that he could heal himself, not faith that if his belief were strong enough his sickness would leave him, but faith that what Christ said was true.

"The cripple believed he could walk, if Jesus said he could. The Bible says in Verse 9, 'And immediately the man was made whole, and took up his bed, and walked.' He believed that what Christ said was true and acted upon it, although all appearances around him indicated that he was still sick. When he *acted* upon the Word of Christ, he was healed."

Christ's Commands Contain His Power to Perform
I continued. "Mary and John, here is the vital key for you to quit smoking. The Bible says, 'Through faith we understand that the worlds were framed by the word of God, so that things which are seen were not made of things which do appear' (Heb. 11:3). The things which are seen were made by the spoken word of God. God said, 'Let there be light,' and golden shafts filtered through the sky. God said, 'Let the dry land appear' and dark, rich earth arose. God said, 'Let birds fly,' and hummingbirds fluttered backwards and forward; 'let animals be placed upon the earth,' and horses galloped and lions roared. 'God spoke and it was done; God commanded, and it stood fast' (Ps. 33:6, 9). The *spoken* word of God carried with it such energy that the audible word became tangible matter.

"Now, the Bible is the *written* Word of God. God's commands and God's promises in His written Word contain God's power as surely as did His spoken word at Creation. What His spoken word said then, He had power to perform. What His written Word says now, He still has power to perform. Every command of Christ's contains His power to perform it.

"Christ's *command* for smokers? 'I beseech you therefore, brethren, by the mercies of God, that ye present your bodies a living sacrifice, holy, acceptable unto God, which is your reasonable service' (Rom. 12:1). Christ's *promise* for smokers? That you might say, 'I can do all things through Christ which strengtheneth me' (Phil. 4:13). Christ's every command contains His promise of power to follow it.

"Now where is your confidence? Is it in the 'I can do all things,' or is it in the phrase *'through Christ* which strengtheneth me'? I John 5:14 tells us, 'And this is the confidence that we have in him, that, if we ask any thing according to his will, he heareth us.' Notice it does not say, 'anything except quite smoking.' So faith is confidence that what God has said in His Word is accompanied by the power to perform it. And since God has said that you can do all things through Him who strengthens you, you can have the confidence that if you ask for anything in faith, according to His will, including giving up smoking, you can have it. You receive the power when you receive Jesus. Receiving Him brings, not only pardon for the past, but power for the present and future.

"John and Mary, you can kneel down right here and pray, 'Lord, give us the strength, give us the power to overcome, and know that the power *is* yours. Sure, you may still have some urges, some cravings. Some do, some do not. They may come as the result of nicotine that has been deposited in the cell system. Cigarette smoking is a physical, social, neuromuscular habit. You may have urges to smoke for weeks and months to come. The nicotine may be out of your body in a relatively short time, but there may be a psychological desire to smoke because you have associated it with almost every waking moment of the day. It may be a tranquilizer, a pleasure provider and something to calm your nerves. You have lit up cigarettes more than you have done anything else in your life, even eating. So you may expect some of those urges. God's promise is not always to take away the craving, but always to make available the victory over it.

"Just like that poor crippled man at the pool believed and was made whole. Let's claim the victory in Jesus before we see it. Based on what God says, Mary and John, would you like to kneel here and open your hearts to God, surrender your tobacco to Him, ask Him to give you the power to overcome, and claim by faith, before you get off you knees, that He has given you that power?"

And so we knelt and I prayed a simple prayer. "Dear Lord, thank You for the power that comes in Jesus; thank You for the strength; thank You for the victory that is Mary's and John's today. Thank You that they need never smoke another cigarette. They may have urges, they may have cravings, but God, I know that in Your word and through Jesus Christ the victory is theirs today. By faith we praise You for that victory. In Christ's name. Amen."

Following a discussion such as the above, I offer the following advice:

Seven Secrets to Staying Off Tobacco

1. *Read the promises of God and continue to claim His victory.* When tempted to smoke, look up the following promises: Philippians 4:13; Philippians 4:19; I Corinthians 10:13; Revelation 3:20; John 1:12; I John 5:14; I John 5:4. Now the Bible says in James 4:7, "Submit yourselves therefore to God. Resist the devil, and he will flee from you." You have submitted yourself to God. But it is necessary for you to resist the devil, because your power of choice is constantly before you. Do this, first of all, by focusing your mind on Jesus, His love for you, and His will for your life.

2. *The second secret is to destroy all of your tobacco.* You are now a non-smoker, and if you keep tobacco around, it is going to be easier for you to yield to the temptation to smoke. So gather up all your tobacco under your bed, in your purse, the closet, the car. Get rid of it if you really mean business. This, too, is resisting the devil.

3. *Drink 10 glasses of water and unfermented fruit juice a day.* Put as much fluid into your system as possible. Buy plenty of your favorite fruit juices—apple, orange, grape, etc. Your kidneys may think it is Christmas and New Year's on the same day! But the idea is to flush the poisons out of your system. For the first 24 hours cut down on your eating, sticking mainly to fruits and some whole grains, but remember to drink plenty of fruit juice. We are resisting the devil.

4. *When you get an overwhelming craving, take a walk.* Breathe deeply, with head erect, shoulder back. The oxygen will help to calm your nerves and get you over the desire to smoke. You need to bathe yourself on the inside with liquid and on the outside with air.

5. *If the desire for a smoke becomes overwhelming, get in the shower.* It is terribly difficult to smoke in the shower! Take a warm and then cool shower. You will feel a calmness in your nerves.

6. *Get to bed earlier than usual.* You may feel on edge. You will need extra sleep to keep you calm.

7. *Avoid caffeine and cola drinks.* Caffeine and nicotine both contain alkaloids so caffeine will stimulate your desire to smoke.

Stop Pleading—Start Praising

The Word of God declares in I Corinthians 15:57, "Thanks be to God, which giveth us the victory through our Lord Jesus Christ." God has given you the victory. Thank Him.

When you pray, do not pray, "Oh, God, please give me the victory." There are some who pray that prayer for weeks, months, years and still smoke. It is the same with any evil in our lives. Never focus on the problem. Concentrate on the solution.

Pray, "Dear Lord, I know that Your power is in my life. I praise You for the victory already given me. I praise You for enabling me to be victorious through You in the future. I believe that what You say is so, accept it as so, and praise You for having made it so in *my* life." Stop pleading start praising.

The principles, illustrated in this chapter through my counsel with Mary and John, apply not only to tobacco, but to every bad habit. The secret to victory over sinful habits can be summed up in four steps: (1) conviction that the habit is sinful, (2) surrender of the habit through submission of the will to Christ, (3) faith that God's call to surrender is accompanied by power for victory, and (4) claim that victory in your life and praise God for it.

Many a person struggles in defeat, surrendering his habits but never claiming the victory already provided. Remember this—Christ has already conquered. He is already victorious. Therefore, victory comes as I lay my sins at His feet, claim the victory that He achieved over Satan, and reach out for the clean slate that He claims for me before the throne of God. All victory comes by faith in the power of the resurrected Christ to strengthen me. My mind is not on my weakness. My mind is on the power of Christ. This is the key to victory.

Continuing Education Assignment

1. Discuss the relationship between Jesus healing the crippled man, and overcoming tobacco.

2. Is the victory over smoking dependent upon deliverance from the craving to smoke?

3. List and memorize the seven secrets of staying off tobacco. Hopefully they will come in handy real soon.

Conclusion

We have considered the essential ingredients necessary to lead men and women to make meaningful decisions for Christ and the Third Angel's Message. Yet technique, apart from your personal commitment to Christ, is like the dry bones of Ezekiel's parable. It is the living Spirit of God in the heart of soul winners that enables them to become effective workers for God. This passion for souls, developed by the inner presence of the Spirit, has characterized all true soul winners. For them, soul winning was not one of many options in life—it was life's central purpose.

George Whitfield, the famous English evangelist, said, "Oh, Lord, give me souls or take my soul." Henry Martin, missionary, standing on India's coral strand cried out, "Here let me burn out for God." Dwight L. Moody of Chicago said, "Use me then, my Saviour, for whatever purpose and whatever way Thou mayest require."

As a young missionary candidate, John MacKenzie knelt on the banks of the Lottie River and prayed, "Oh, Lord, send me to the darkest spot on earth." Mrs. Comstock, missionary in India, while sending her children home prayed, "Lord Jesus, I do this for thee." John Hunt, a missionary to the Fiji Islands, prayed on his deathbed, "Lord, save Fiji, save these people; Oh Lord, have mercy on Fiji."

David Brainard, a celebrated missionary, while laboring among the poor, benighted Indians of Delaware said, "I care not where I live or what hardships I go through so that I can but gain souls to Christ. While I'm asleep, I dream of these things. As soon as I awake, the first thing I think of is the great work."

When General William Booth, at 75 years of age, was invited to Buckingham Palace by Edward VII, he summed up his life's work by writing in the king's guest book, "Your Majesty, some men's ambition is art, some men's ambition is fame, some men's ambition is gold. But my ambition is the souls of men."

Ellen White echoed these sentiments:

> *The work above all work—the business above all others which should draw and engage the energies of the soul—is the work of saving souls for whom Christ has died. Make this the main, the important work of your life. Make it your special life work.*
> —*The Youth's Instructor*, May 4, 1893

A passion for souls is not something that is worked up. It is rather something that is sent down from above. A burden for souls is not merely inspired by the thought of personal success— it is inspired by a view of Calvary.

As we come to grips with the fact that when Jesus comes men and women are either saved or lost, that for them it is heaven or hell; as we come to realize that our influence does count, that we can make a difference in the lives of others, that through our actions the Holy Spirit can more powerfully work to save others, we are thus motivated to participate with Christ in the most glorious work in the world.

Friend of mine, as you have read the pages of this book, it is the deep desire of my heart that the things we have said are more than simply techniques, but that you will adopt these living principles into your ministry and become a more effective soul winner for Christ. Not merely so that your name will appear in the pages of church papers as a mighty soul winner, but so that you will have the joy of more effectively cooperating with Christ in helping others.

Sensing that God wants to use you as His spokesperson to reach out to the lost, will you not this very day kneel in a deeper commitment to Jesus, inviting His Spirit to take full possession of you? Will you not ask God to open your eyes to lost men and women around you? Will you not ask Him to give you greater results in your ministry? Will you not ask Him to place within your heart, by means of His Holy Spirit, a deeper burden for souls? Will you not kneel right now wherever you are reading this book, and pray this simple prayer:

"Dear Lord, grant me a passion for souls. Help me to see men and women as Jesus saw them—potential candidates for the kingdom of heaven. Grant, me, in the light of the cross, the desire to cooperate with Him in the most wonderful work in the world— the work of redemption. May I be totally possessed with the Holy Spirit so that nothing in my life will keep me from effectively working for others.

"And Father, may we work side by side. I am weak, I am at times fearful that I will not succeed. But in faith and absolute confidence I dedicate myself to You, knowing You will use me. I thank You. In Christ's name. Amen."

Bibliography

Anderson, Roy Allen. *The Shepherd Evangelist*. Washington D.C.: Review and Herald Pub Assn.,1950.

Coon, Glenn A. *A Path to the Heart*. Hagerstown, Md.: Review and Herald Pub. Assn., 1958.

Coleman, E. Robert. *The Master Plan of Evangelism*. Fleming Revell Co.

Detamore, Fordyce, *Seeking His Lost Sheep*, Collegedale, Tenn.: Southern Pub. Assn., 1965.

Eims, Leroy. *Winning Ways*. Wheaton, Ill.: Victor Books, 1977.

Fish, R. J. *Giving a Good Invitation*. Nashville, Tenn: Broadman Press, 1975

Ford, Leighton. "The Evangelistic Invitation" *Leadership* Fall 1984

Graham, Billy. *Billy Graham Speaks*. New York: Roset & Dunlip, 1968.

Gray, Donald. *Lay Bible Workers' Manual*. Berrien Springs, Mich.: Lake Union Conference of Seventh-day Adventists.

Griffin, Em. *The Mind Changers*. Wheaton, Ill.: Tyndale House Publ 1976.

Koller, Charles. *Expository Preaching Without Notes*. Grand Rapids, Mich.: Baker Book House, 1962.

McDill,Wayne. *Making Friends For Christ*. Nashville, Tenn: Broadman Press.

McPhee, Arthur. *Friendship Evangelism*. Harrisonburg, Va.: Choice Books, 1978.

Shuler, John L. *Public Evangelism*. Hagerstown, Md.: Review and Herald Pub. Assn., 1940.

Spurgeon The Soul Winner. Grand Rapids, Mich.: 1963.

Street, R. Alan. *The Effective Invitation*. New Jersey: Fleming M. Revell Co.

Tan, Paul Lee. *Encyclopedia of 7700 Illustrations*. Rockville, Md.: Assurance Publishers.

Wearner, Alonzo J. *The Art of Personal Evangelism*. Hagerstown, Md.: Review and Herald Pub. Assn., 1934.

White, Ellen G. *Evangelism* and *Gospel Workers*. Hagerstown, Md.: Review and Herald Pub. Assn., 1934.

White, Ellen G. *Manuscript 4*. 1893.

White, Ellen G. *Testimonies*. Mountain View, Calif.: Pacific Press Pub. Assn.

Wiggins, Kembleton. *Soul Winning Made Easier*. Mountain View, Calif.: Pacific Press Publ Assn., 1975.

Woolsey, Raymond. *Evangelism Handbook*. Hagerstown, Md.: Review and Herald Pub. Assn., 1972.